THE GIFT
OF TIME

Also Available from Dorset House Publishing

Becoming a Technical Leader: An Organic Problem-Solving Approach
by Gerald M. Weinberg
ISBN: 978-0-932633-02-6   Copyright © 1986   304 pages, softcover

Exploring Requirements: Quality Before Design
by Gerald M. Weinberg and Donald C. Gause
ISBN: 978-0-932633-13-2   Copyright © 1989   320 pages, softcover

General Principles of Systems Design
by Gerald M. Weinberg and Daniela Weinberg
ISBN: 978-0-932633-07-1   Copyright © 1988   376 pages, softcover

Handbook of Walkthroughs, Inspections, and Technical Reviews, 3rd ed.
by Gerald M. Weinberg and Daniel P. Freedman
ISBN: 978-0-932633-19-4   Copyright © 1990   464 pages, softcover

An Introduction to General Systems Thinking: Silver Anniversary Edition
by Gerald M. Weinberg
ISBN: 978-0-932633-49-1   Copyright © 2001   304 pages, softcover

More Secrets of Consulting: The Consultant's Tool Kit
by Gerald M. Weinberg
ISBN: 978-0-932633-52-1   Copyright © 2002   216 pages, softcover

Perfect Software: And Other Illusions About Testing
by Gerald M. Weinberg
ISBN: 978-0-932633-69-9   Copyright © 2008   200 pages, softcover

The Psychology of Computer Programming: Silver Anniversary Edition
by Gerald M. Weinberg
ISBN: 978-0-932633-42-2   Copyright © 1998   360 pages, softcover

Weinberg on Writing: The Fieldstone Method
by Gerald M. Weinberg
ISBN: 978-0-932633-65-1   Copyright © 2006   208 pages, softcover

---

For More Information

✔ Contact us for prices, shipping options, availability, and more.

✔ Sign up to receive *INSIDE DORSET HOUSE (iDH)* by mail or fax.

✔ Send e-mail to subscribe to *iDH,* our e-mail newsletter.

✔ Visit Dorsethouse.com for savings, reviews, downloads, and more.

DORSET HOUSE PUBLISHING
An Independent Publisher of Books on
Systems and Software Development and Management. Since 1984.
3143 Broadway, Suite 2B   New York, NY 10027   USA
1-800-DH-BOOKS   1-800-342-6657
212-620-4053   fax: 212-727-1044
info@dorsethouse.com   www.dorsethouse.com

THE GIFT OF TIME

Essays in Honor of
Gerald M. Weinberg,
on His 75th Birthday

edited by Fiona Charles

DORSET HOUSE PUBLISHING
3143 BROADWAY, SUITE 2B
NEW YORK, NEW YORK 10027

12 11 10 9 8 7 6 5 4 3 2 1

Acknowledgments

I am grateful to everyone who helped make this book happen. My thanks go first to Wendy Eakin of Dorset House, for her enthusiastic reception and support of both the original idea and the subsequent proposal. A most heartfelt thank-you goes to all the contributors, who met very tight deadlines with cheerful grace, and—more importantly—with solidly fine work. Naomi Karten gave much encouragement and valuable advice, especially at the beginning when I was very green. Sherry Heinze not only put up with my incessant excitement as I signed up contributors, but then helped with the copyediting and other details. Dani Weinberg supplied precious photographs from her life with Jerry. And last, but never least, Jill Shefrin read, criticized, advised, and supported me from the first early notion to the finished book.

Selecting contributors for a work of this nature is necessarily subjective, and even arbitrary. Jerry's huge community includes many accomplished writers, thinkers, teachers, and practitioners. I could not ask them all, so I elected to invite professional writers, mainly, and people whose work encompasses themes and concepts representing the range of Jerry's work. I know there are many others who would have loved to contribute. I regret that space and the logistical challenges of pulling the book together prevented including them all, and I hope for their forgiveness.

Contents

Preface

This book celebrates Gerald M. Weinberg for the time that he has given to the Information Technology world. In an astonishing career spanning fifty-plus years, Jerry (as he is known to many) is author of more than forty published nonfiction books, many of them enormously influential, and (to date) one novel. Through those years, he built and ran a successful consulting business, and he designed and taught courses that helped to change his students' lives.

Jerry's career has been so long that it is sometimes easy to forget just what a pioneer he has always been. He had the extraordinary good fortune to be in the right place at the right time, launching his career at the dawn of commercial computing. When IBM first began shipping computers to its customers, Jerry—the programmer—went right along with them.

Though he may not have invented Information Technology consulting as a profession, Jerry was one of its first and best practitioners, pioneering methods and techniques that many consultants now take for granted. The experiential courses he designed with his wife, Dani, and other collaborators—such as Don Gause and Jean McLendon—were unique and have remained so, famous for their quality and power to effect positive change in their participants.

In the 1990s, Jerry was the moving spirit behind Consultant's Camp, an annual week-long gathering for consultants to share learning, and starting in 1998, his moderated online forum, SHAPE (for *Software* as a *Human Activity Performed Effectively*), carried lively and valuable exchanges for ten years, generating two books of discussion along the way.[1] In 2000, he contributed his vast knowledge of experiential learning to the founding and cohosting of the annual Amplifying Your Effectiveness (AYE) Conference. With its half-day experiential sessions, skilled presenters, and limited number of participants, AYE offers a learning experience like no other conference.

Jerry's most influential work has focused on the human side of software development, with which he has had extensive experience as a programmer, project manager, and consultant. His work synthesizes and extends concepts and practices from his own wide-ranging experiences and from explorations in diverse areas, including the psychology of problem solving, general systems thinking, Virginia Satir's family therapy, the Myers-Briggs personality preference model, experiential learning, anthropology, and dog training.

His output has been prolific, and it remains so. He is still writing and teaching, though he has cut back a little on some kinds of work; he generally prefers now to propagate his authorial voice through fiction. Jerry still participates as a host and presenter at the annual AYE Conference, and has recently revived his Problem Solving Leadership course after a hiatus of some years. Jerry and his work continue to have a profound and far-reaching influence on his students and readers.

As is fitting in a volume celebrating the work of a uniquely influential thinker and practitioner, this collection contains a mixture of reminiscence, analysis, and technique. There are biographical pieces by three of Jerry's decades-long colleagues— Robert L. Glass, Jean McLendon, and Dani Weinberg. I invited other contributors to select and write about a concept or technique they adopted or adapted from Jerry or his work, a topic that's central to their own work, perhaps synthesized with their own experiences and learnings into something that is uniquely their own.

I faced an interesting challenge in deciding how to sequence the essays. One early thought was to map the topics to a rough chronology of Jerry's work. Or I could group related topics together. In the end, I decided that Jerry's output represents an integrated body of thought, and that integration is reflected in many of these essays. So, I ordered them in what seemed to me a pleasing and coherent sequence for someone reading cover-to-cover.

Each contribution touches on a different aspect of Jerry's work and influence, and displays a different perspective. For example, Bob Glass, Jerry's almost-exact contemporary, gives us a fifty-year overview and—amusingly—tells us of memorable interactions he has had with Jerry. Author of many influential books about software development and project management, Bob is the book's most seasoned contributor.

Next, James Bach describes Jerry as the pioneer software tester. In so doing, James reveals much about how he himself thinks about and practices testing, and he shares an essential source of ideas in the development of his own work.

Michael Bolton's piece, about the important critical thinking and questioning skills he learned from Jerry, follows.

Next are three essays dealing primarily with the application of Satir models and techniques, preceded by an interview with therapist and business consultant Jean McLendon, past president of the Virginia Satir Global Network. In the interview, Jean describes meeting the Weinbergs and working with them to design and conduct the program that became the Congruent Leadership Change Shop.

In the first essay on Satir techniques, Sue Petersen gives a new twist to the idea of rules and rule transformations, among other Satir techniques for creating tools that enhance self-esteem and help in dealing with problems between people.

In the second, Esther Derby describes how to give congruent feedback that improves working relationships.

In the final essay of this group, Willem van den Ende shows how he uses Satir concepts and a diagram of effects to solve a difficult problem encountered in working with groups.

The remaining essays defy easy categorization.

Judah Mogilensky conveys how he uses his observations of behavior to augment the official data required in Capability Maturity Model Integration appraisals, and to predict the success of a process improvement initiative.

In an essay on the wisdom and value of experiential learning, Naomi Karten draws on her own ideas and extensive experience in designing and leading experiential workshops, as well as the years she spent co-instructing the Problem Solving Leadership with Jerry and learning from him.

Next is James Bullock's reflection on the Problem Solving Leadership course from the participant's point of view, in which he compares the PSL experience with the practice and learning of Aikido.

Tim Lister relates how he first encountered Jerry's written words as a young programmer in his first IT job. He describes the influence that Jerry's books have had on his thinking since then— during his more than thirty years as a consultant.

Johanna Rothman describes techniques Jerry taught her to overcome writer's block and how she adapted them, added others, while becoming the author of three books and many articles.

Recognizing that most of us contributors occupy what one SHAPE member calls "middle youth," I decided the book needed the balance of a younger perspective. Jerry's work has affected more than one generation, so I asked Jonathan Kohl, our youngest contributor, to explore that. He writes about how he, his contemporaries, and younger colleagues continue to learn and apply techniques from Jerry's work to solve problems encountered in their own practices.

Either of the next two pieces could have made a fitting end to the book. I decided to put Dani Weinberg's wonderful reflection on her life and work partnership with Jerry second-to-last. Dani describes her many career changes in concert with Jerry's career, not least her consulting days with Weinberg and Weinberg and her work in codesigning and teaching PSL and Congruent Leadership Change Shop.

Finally, Bent Adsersen's essay on time—what it means and how to get it—ends the book, with the "gift of time" theme.

In his consulting, and perhaps even more in his teaching, Jerry has affected the lives of many—and not just their working lives.

In my own career, I came very early—and very late—to Jerry's work. In 1978, I landed a summer job as a technical writer at my university's library automation company, on the tenuous grounds that I knew nothing whatever about computers but, as an English major, must know how to write. On my first day, I acquired two valuable tools: an open ticket to the computer science library, where I might find books to learn the job, and a loaner copy of *The Psychology of Computer Programming*, to "understand the people you're going to be working with."

That first job gave me a mission to help users of systems, and an abiding faith in the capacity of software to make their lives better—if we can only get it right. By the end of the summer, I had fallen deeply in love, with both software and the milieu we develop it in. That sense of purpose and that love were due in no small part to my avid reading of *The Psychology of Computer Programming*, which taught me from the first day to observe, seek to understand, and work with human interactions.

I never forgot my delight in that book, but at the time I couldn't afford to buy my own copy. It was not until I joined a computer book club in the early nineties and embarked on an intensive reading program that I rediscovered Jerry's writing. Over the next few years, I devoured as many of Jerry's books as I could, starting with *Are Your Lights On?* and *Exploring Requirements: Quality Before Design. Handbook of Walkthroughs, Inspections, and Technical Reviews* became a bible for my QA team. And, as they became available, I scooped up each of the four volumes of *Quality Software Management.* Then, in 1998, I finally acquired *The Psychology of Computer Programming,* in the silver anniversary edition.

It never occurred to me that I could meet the man and study with him. But in a chance conversation at a conference, James Bach pointed me to Jerry's Website. Of course, I have some regrets I didn't find it earlier. But when I saw the description of Jerry's Problem Solving Leadership course on his site, it was the right time for me, and I persuaded my employer to send me to the next class.

My PSL began, as do all PSLs, on a Sunday evening with an introductory dinner. On Monday, we were presented with all sorts of problems to solve, and worked in teams of varying sizes. I enjoyed it immensely. Rising early Tuesday morning to swim before breakfast, I found the swimming pool locked up. Mildly annoyed, I went for a walk instead, in Albuquerque Old Town. It was a glorious morning for a walk, bright and clear, in the magically breathable New Mexico air. I returned to the hotel happily anticipating the day's class.

It was the morning of September 11, 2001.

I came into the room reserved for PSL breakfast, and greeted the two women there: an American and a Belgian. Looking at me strangely, one of them said, "You don't know what's happening, do you?" I waited. The American woman burst out, "We're under attack!"

Now, I am a Canadian, of Anglo-Scottish extraction. Drama is not my first resort. But as I stood there, fragments of thought tumbled through my mind: "American hyperbole! But . . . this is a problem-solving leadership course. Is this a simulation? No! That would be unethical. Jerry wouldn't do that!"

I had met the man over dinner Sunday and had spent a single day in his class, solving problems and listening to him talk, and already I knew that about him. I knew it absolutely.

All right, then. This is for real, I thought. *Where do we go from here?*

More people came in and shared what they had heard so far or seen on television. It was horrific.

We went into class and sat down: a circle of shocked and frightened people. Jerry started to talk. Almost the first thing he said was, "We don't know very much yet. We'll find out more as the day goes on, but in the meantime, let us not assume that this is from outside. It could just as easily be some nut from Montana who doesn't want to pay income tax."

For me, that was an anchor: the single best thing anyone could have said. Don't assume anything. Don't go rushing about panicking. Ask questions. Be patient until you have data. Jerry's gentle, authoritative, and reasonable tone steadied us.

We learned more as the morning went on, of course. It was indeed an attack from outside. Jerry made room for people to take care of their personal needs, call their families or employers, whatever they needed to do. He talked all morning, quietly, steadily, calmly.

Just when I was starting to think, "If this man says one more word, I'm going to have to get up and start throwing chairs around!" Jerry suddenly said, "We need to do something physical. Does everyone know how to do a knot?"

He invited us to join him in the middle of the room. With eyes closed, we thrust our hands into the center of the group and grasped any wrist we could reach. We opened our eyes to a seemingly impenetrable tangle: twenty-odd people knotted together by hand and wrist. Then we untangled, slowly, without letting go—working together, segment by segment.

It was exactly what we needed: physical activity, combined with an amusing and absorbing problem. And near-strangers reaped the comfort of physical contact with other humans without intrusive intimacy. (Like all PSL activities, participation in the knot was optional. But nobody chose to opt out.)

With his co-instructor, Naomi Karten, Jerry resumed "normal" PSL activities, but always over the ground bass of 9/11 and its aftermath. For me, a sojourner in a foreign country under a state of emergency, Jerry was a rock: a voice of sanity and reason in a wildly—even dangerously—irrational world.

PSL must always have been an intense experience for those who were open to all it offered. This one—the 9/11 PSL—was especially intense. Naomi revisits this day later in this volume, from her perspective as co-instructor.

Jerry's generosity with his own time is well-known among his students and friends. In the closing chapter of this book, Bent Adsersen relates how Jerry once told him that time is the most valuable gift one person can give to another. Author, mentor, writing coach, consultant, storyteller, and friend, Jerry has freely given that most valuable gift, often and to many.

The contributors to this volume have all been recipients of that gift. As readers, students, clients, colleagues, friends—and wife, in Dani Weinberg's case—we have shared precious time with Jerry, gaining much from the exchange.

This book is a gift of time we give to Jerry: from a few of his many students, friends, colleagues, and his publisher, an offering in celebration of his seventy-fifth birthday.

THE GIFT
OF TIME

1

Personal Recollections of and a Biographical Look at Jerry Weinberg, Computing and Software Pioneer

Robert L. Glass

"Gerald M. Weinberg" cites the formal material describing him, but *Jerry Weinberg* is how most of us know him.

Jerry is a towering figure in the world of computing and software. He has written more than three-dozen books on the subject, most of them seen to be among the most important books published on the topic he has chosen. The total number of his publications (including papers and articles) runs up close to four hundred. For more than forty years now, Jerry is arguably the most visible person in our field, and unarguably, he is among the top half-dozen.

Jerry's academic record speaks for itself. Like that of many software pioneers, Jerry's degree—in 1955, a B.S. at the University of Nebraska—was not in computing subject matter (there were no schools offering such degrees back then), and his majors were, instead, physics and math. A year later, he enrolled to obtain his M.A. in physics at Cal-Berkeley. He then tried his hand at industry practice: at IBM and later on at NASA, working on Project Mercury, before returning to school for his Ph.D. in communications sciences from the University of Michigan, in 1965. It is worthwhile to note, once again, that all of this happened before there were such things as computer science academic programs and computer science degrees. Communications Sciences was about the most computer-relevant field you could find in the mid 1960s!

Before I write more specifically about Jerry's accomplishments, however, I want to share some personal chapters in my knowledge of Jerry. Jerry and I have interacted infrequently over the years, which is perhaps surprising in a community as tightly focused as ours. But each of those interactions has been, in very diverse ways, exceedingly memorable to me.

The first had to do with something Jerry wrote. It was an article, decades ago, that became one of the most influential pieces I have ever read in the software field. The specifics of the article have long ago vanished in the mists of my memories of the past, but I will never forget the gist of what he presented there. He was describing the publication of what became, more than thirty-five years ago, the first best-selling book in the computing field: *The Psychology of Computer Programming* (PCP). But what was memorable about that article was not about *PCP* as a success story—it was about *PCP* as a failure story. In that article, Jerry told the story of his initial attempts to get the book published. It suffered rejection after rejection, as publishers were either (a) unable to figure out what it was good for, or (b) thought it was far too narrowly focused. (As I recall, one publisher referred to it as a "one-trick pony.") But Jerry continued submitting the manuscript until persistence paid off and it was accepted for publication, eventually becoming the dramatic success for which it is better known. I've remembered that lesson through the years, as I have sometimes struggled to get some of my own work published.

The second memorable interaction happened in Tokyo, back in 1982. Jerry was the keynoter that year at the International Conference on Software Engineering. The content of his presentation was indeed memorable, as I am sure he intended it to be; I was very impressed, I recall, by the points he was making to his international audience of top software professionals and academics. But what I remember most clearly is that Jerry wore to his presentation one of the loudest Hawaiian shirts I had ever seen! I have wondered many times since why Jerry did that. Was it to announce to the world that he was an informal kind of guy? Did he want to convey some kind of variant on "beauty is only skin deep," that content is more important than style and form? Or

4

perhaps was his luggage late in arriving in Tokyo, and he had to wear what he had worn on the plane?

Now, I realize that computing folk are seldom known for their sartorial splendor. On a personal level, I am known for my own informality in dress. Because of that, I really do apply the personally pertinent expression, "People who live in Glass houses shouldn't throw stones." But still, I do hope that I will someday come to understand that memorable moment of Jerry in his Hawaiian shirt!

The third memorable moment isn't really about a memory, nor is it about a moment that I can be confident actually occurred. It has to do with my learning that Jerry was a physics and math dual-major at the University of Nebraska, graduating with his degree in 1955. During that period, he apparently was invited to join the math honorary society Pi Mu Epsilon. Now, here's where it gets peculiar and tenuous: I, too, was a math major back in that long-ago era, at Culver-Stockton, an obscure northeast Missouri college. And I, too, was a member of Pi Mu Epsilon. And (to get this story moving forward), we C-S Pi Mu Epsilons traveled to Lincoln to install the newly formed chapter of our society at the University of Nebraska, Lincoln. What strikes me now is that Jerry may very well have been present that installation evening, may have been one of the members of the newly installed chapter that our small team was welcoming to the honorary mathematical world. *Hi, Jerry! Did we meet way back then, when neither of us knew what the future had in store?*

But now, on to the reality of Jerry's accomplishments.

Perhaps surprisingly, *PCP*, that long-ago best-seller, was not Jerry's first publication. Fully a decade earlier, in 1961, his first book was published. It was *Computer Programming Fundamentals*, coauthored with H.D. Leeds, published by McGraw-Hill, and later translated into Japanese. I dwell on this debut because it is notable that not much was happening in the formal world of software development back in those days. Academic computer science and information systems were not to happen for another half-dozen years, and academic software engineering was a couple of decades in the future. Although the profession of software development, as opposed to its academic presence, was already almost a decade old at that point, here was Jerry, marching ahead of a parade that had not quite formed!

Moreover, that book was not even Jerry's first appearance on the public computing scene. His paper "Pipeline Network Analysis by Electronic Digital Computer" was published in (of all places!) the application-domain-focused *Journal of the American Water Works Association*, in 1957. Way back then, most of today's software folks were hardly even a gleam in their parents' eyes. *All of you who have read "Pipeline Network Analysis," please raise your hands!* I suspect there are zero hands raised among the readers of this volume.

Nine years after that first book's publication, when the maturation of the computing field was much further along, Jerry and Herb Leeds brought out a new edition: *Computer Programming Fundamentals Based on the IBM System 360*. This was probably an opportunistic coup on their part. The three-sixty, the field-changing hardware that replaced all of IBM's previous computer lines, came along in the mid-1960s and was a major milestone in the history of the computing field. By the second edition's 1970 publication date, the three-sixty had become the computer of choice for most computer organizations in practice. (It was said "You can't get fired for buying IBM" back in those IBM-monopolistic days.) Relating the earlier book to this new, dominant hardware line was a natural.

That is not to say, of course, that this was the peak of Jerry's publishing story. It was only a year later that *The Psychology of Computer Programming* came out, quickly becoming the first bestseller in the computing field. In the same way that his first book was republished in a later version, *PCP* was to emerge—in a silver anniversary edition—in 1998, published by Dorset House, by then his long-time publisher. The first edition of *PCP* became, in many ways, the beginning of Jerry's golden age of book authorship. Between then and the mid-1980s, more books emerged. There was *An Introduction to General Systems Thinking* (1975) and, with Daniel P. Freedman, *Handbook of Walkthroughs, Inspections, and Technical Reviews* (1977), which became arguably the most important contribution to the well-published field of inspection/review books. Next came *On the Design of Stable Systems* (1979), written with Jerry's wife and partner, Dani, reissued under the title *General Prin-*

ciples of Systems Design (1988); *Are Your Lights On?* written with Don Gause (1982); *Understanding the Professional Programmer* (1982); and, in 1985, *The Secrets of Consulting*, Jerry's first book published by Dorset House.

Some of Jerry's best writing was yet to come in the 1990s and beyond, starting with his four-volume *Quality Software Management* (QSM) series, which emerged over five years from 1992 to 1997. Reviewers loved *QSM* for bringing together, in published form, Jerry's most important ideas about software quality and technical leadership, forming a comprehensive treatise on how to achieve true quality.

Most recently, Jerry joined the select few of computing people who have broadened their interest in technical writing to the field of novels. I think of people who move in that direction— Tom DeMarco is another—as the "Renaissance Folk" of the computing field. It is fairly daring for a technical expert to publish in the field of fiction. Jerry's first published novel, *The Aremac Project* (2007), may not win a Nobel prize, but it is a good read, with enough suspense and a surprise ending to keep the reader engrossed. The back cover mentions that Jerry was (at the time) at work on his sixth novel, and I have no doubt Jerry's early experience in fighting to succeed in getting *PCP* published will come into play again here.

In his early years, sometimes writing with coauthors, Jerry dabbled in the category of "how-to" books. There was one on the PL/I programming language, in 1966; one on structured programming with PL/C, in 1973; and one on COBOL, in 1977. More recently, Jerry gave readers a different kind of how-to book, *Weinberg on Writing* (2006), a personal discussion of a subject with which Jerry is clearly extremely familiar. (That book went on to be named a finalist for the Jolt, a prominent annual award in computing.)

Most of what Jerry has written is solid, referenceable, respectable material, often serving as a most important contribution to whatever subject he has chosen. There are occasional exceptions to that rule, of course, and controversy occasionally arises in the wake of Jerry's works.

My favorite controversy arose in the context of Jerry's definition and defense of what he called egoless programming in that early-on *PCP* book. Egoless programming, of course, has a lot going for it. The idea (in case you haven't taken part in this controversy over the years) was that programmers needed to program as members of a team, not as independent cowboys. (The cowboy culture was still pretty dominant when Jerry wrote *PCP*.) An egoless programmer was one who was proud of his team's product, independently of how proud he was of his own work on that product.

That thought always bothered me. Of course, programmers must be proud of their team and proud of their team's product. But at the same time, I always felt, they needed at least as much to be proud of their own individual contribution to that team and that product. The best programmers, I strongly felt, were the ones who felt good about their technology, felt good about their work, and felt good about the products they produced.

As I mulled over the apparent contradiction between egoless programming and my own strongly felt notion of the proud programmer, I conceived an analogy. Imagine, I said at the time, the notion of an egoless programming manager. If egoless programming is good, isn't egoless management even better? And yet, it is nearly impossible for most of us to conceive of something that could be called an egoless manager. It simply makes no sense—the contribution of the manager is too intimately tied to his personal ego to imagine the alternative. And if egoless management makes no sense, shouldn't we say the same thing about egoless programming?

Jerry addressed this controversy in his silver anniversary edition of *PCP*, published by Dorset House in 1998. There, he cites this as the "most misunderstood . . . concept . . . in the original book," suggesting that perhaps he should have proclaimed "less ego" instead of "egoless."

The controversy eventually simmered down and dissolved into obscurity, as well it should have. Jerry was right, of course, that the team aspects of egoless programming were vitally important for programmers to absorb, especially in the era of the programmer as cowboy. But, I would still maintain, you separate the ego of any professional from his performance at your peril. Feeling good about what you personally have done is too important to all of us to ignore its impact.

Quibbles aside, when it comes to book authorship, few compete with Jerry on quantity, and none compete with him on quality and quantity combined. Most importantly, none compete with his writing for influence on the emerging field of computing and software. The topics Jerry has chosen to address impressively span the spectrum of possible software subjects, ranging from the software life cycle to general systems thinking to human factors to management and leadership. His influence on the field has been both deep and broad.

But there has been much more to Jerry than book authorship. In his professional career, he has been self-employed as a consultant and facilitator for thirty-five years; he was a professor (at the University of Nebraska, International College, and SUNY/Binghamton); and he was an industry practitioner (mostly at various branches of IBM).

His list of consulting clients is nearly as long as his publication list, including, predictably, many of the leading companies in the computing field. But there is a diversity of other industry domains, from utilities to banking to autos to insurance. And there's a strong number of governments, particularly U.S. state governments, represented as well. Jerry is clearly among the pioneers of IT consulting. He is certainly high up on the list of those with a diversity of focus. And, with Dani, a cultural anthropologist, he has been able to bring a unique dimension to his consulting work.

Jerry's books, writings, and consulting have had a profound effect on the computing field, of course. So, too, have the dozens of keynote addresses he has presented at conferences over the years.

But perhaps his strongest influences on the field have come from the series of courses and conferences that he has helped to bring into being and hosted, with various collaborators (including Jean McLendon and Dani). Myriads have benefited from the intensive experiential learning embodied in the Problem Solving Leadership and Congruent Leadership Change Shop workshops, as well as his System Effectiveness Management program, often describing their impact as "life-changing." In 2000, Jerry joined with a group of fellow consultants to found and cohost the Amplifying Your Effectiveness conference. AYE conferences, which continue annually, are revered among their attendees as highly motivating, more-than-just-educational events, the highlight of the year. I often wonder whether Jerry, the host and experiential session-leader at these AYE conferences, wears a Hawaiian shirt!

So, there we have it. Gerald M. Weinberg. Computing and software pioneer. Keynoter, teacher, conference host. Author of major, influential books. Frequently published author of technical papers. Influential and effective consultant. One of the most important—and one of the nicest—people in the computing and software profession!

Happy seventy-fifth birthday, Jerry!

The Prince of Testers

James Bach

I knew he wouldn't be able to resist. That's why I set up just ten feet from Jerry's booth. His keynote speech had gone well, and now he was sitting at a Meet the Experts table. Conferees drifted by to ask questions and get a bit of free consulting, but I wanted Jerry's attention for myself. Since I didn't want to ask him to shirk his duty to the conference, my plan was to entice him to shirk—*without* having to ask.

So, I challenged another software tester to solve a problem— one that I often pose as part of my coaching practice. It's a card game that resembles the classic Mastermind game, with some twists that make it an open-ended opportunity for experimentation. This is relevant to training testers because each test of a real software product is a kind of experiment. The two of us made a production out of moving a table toward where Jerry sat, getting chairs, and setting out the playing cards and note paper. I explained the rules and the tester got started.

It was only a few minutes before a shadow suddenly loomed over us.

"This looks interesting," Jerry said, hovering, having abandoned his booth, leaving petitioners to wander in the wilderness a little while longer.

"Oh. Hi, Jerry. Nice to see you. We're just playing a little testing game, here. You might like it. It's designed to exercise the skills of experiment design, conjecture and refutation, and observation. Tom's goal is to discover which cards I like and which cards I don't. Maybe . . ." I shrugged elaborately, "you have an idea or two to contribute?"

"Okay, tell me how it works."

"*Exx*-cellent! Here is a pack of ordinary playing cards. What you do is select four cards and show them to me. That's called a 'showing.' If I like a card in your showing, I take it and you don't get it back. If I don't like it, I leave it. You repeatedly show me sets of cards until you think you know the principle I'm using to select the cards. When you've figured that out, show me five cards and declare it as your 'final showing.' If I take each of those five cards, you win."

"Sounds easy enough. Here's my showing." He placed three cards on the table.

"I need to see four cards at a time, Jerry," I said. "Do you want to hear the rules again?"

"There *are* four cards," he replied with comic indignation. Then he pointed at a napkin on the table. "I call that a card."

"No, that is not a card."

"Tell me more about that. It looks like a card to me. It's made of paper. It's flat."

"It has to be a playing card."

"Well then . . ." He scribbled a crude drawing of a Jack of Diamonds on the napkin. "Now there are four cards."

"No, I meant a *real* playing card. From your deck."

"*Ohhhh.* Well, let me see." He picked up the cards and selected four fresh cards from his deck, placing them face down on the table. "Like any of those?"

I reached to turn them face up. "Interesting," mused Jerry as he hastily gathered the cards before I could see them and take any. "You seem to need to see the faces of the cards. That tells me that your algorithm probably has something to do with the semantics of the card faces. Or it could be just your habit. Say, is there another deck around here?"

"Ah, not that I know of, Jerry. Try to focus."

"I just thought if you don't normally look at the backs of the cards, I would slip you a duplicate card from another deck and see what happens. It's not like you would know. But, never mind. Here's another showing." He slapped five cards down in quick succession.

"Is that your final showing?"

"No, it is not."

"Then you must show me only four cards."

"But, James, there *are* only four cards."

"I think I see five cards on the table, Doctor Weinberg."

He gathered the five cards and held up the left-most. "That's a joker. I didn't know that you would consider it a card. Now I do."

If you're not used to it, Jerry's manner of play might seem silly to you, even exasperating. But to me, it was wonderful. Notice how he did not enter the game with strong assumptions about what the rules meant, or how they mattered. He knew that playing the game "straight" would probably cost him some cards, so he began with several strategies to probe the structure of the problem without much risk to his cards. In so doing, he opened himself to learning about many more potential variables than does a more typical player of the game, at a lower cost. He was practicing the first responsibility of a tester.

Knowing That Things Could Be Different

It was Jerry himself who introduced me to that first responsibility, some years before. I had been visiting him for a week of conversation and writing work, and we were heading up his driveway on one of our walks, when abruptly he asked, "What's the first responsibility of a tester?"

My head was immediately brimming with candidates. "I don't think I can pick just one. How about five?"

"I'll tell you what it is," he said, waving me off. "The first responsibility of a tester is to explore and challenge the constraints of the situation. Kind of like how you just challenged the constraints of my question. A tester is someone who knows that things could be different. However they appear, however they really are, whatever we feel about them, it all could be different than it seems, or different tomorrow than it is today. Testers need to be inquisitive; to shake things up a bit, so that people can see things in a different light. Now here's another question for you: What do you do if you don't have enough time to find every bug in a program?"

"That's a trick question. No one ever has the time to find every bug in a program. But that's not our goal. Our goal usually is to find every important bug."

"And if there isn't time to do that?"

"Well, that's why we use our risk analysis to guide us. We put our efforts where they are most needed."

"And if your risk analysis is wrong?"

"That's why we also use a non-risk-oriented test strategy for some of the testing. For instance, we might use a coverage-oriented test technique to scan for unknown risks."

"And if you aren't given enough time to do that well? Or maybe you have the time and you do it badly?"

"I suppose we just keep trying, and we also try to learn from our mistakes."

"True, but you might not learn the right things from your mistakes. Do you see what I'm getting at, James?" I shrugged expectantly and he continued. "Beyond any clever strategy you try, there is something further that you need: You need a philosophy of acceptance."

"A philosophy of acceptance? We just accept failure?"

"You accept reality. That's a tester's job. Your strategies will occasionally fail, no matter what you do. While a tester's first responsibility is to refuse to accept the apparent constraints of the situation, a tester must ultimately accept that some ambiguities and constraints may never be identified or resolved. It's an awkward field. If you wanted solid ground to stand on, you chose the wrong vocation."

I had to smile at that. "Must be why I like it, Jerry. Solvable problems are so tedious."

Testing by Ignoring Testing Problems

Jerry Weinberg is not much known as a tester. He is famous more as a programmer, a teacher of programmers, a systems thinker, a teacher of systems thinkers, a teacher of technical leaders, a writer, a teacher of writers, and—very prominently in recent years—a teacher of teachers. Still, I consider Jerry to be one of the great testers in the history of computing. His work profoundly influences my practice.

As I see it, the reason Jerry is not recognized as a tester is simple. Bluntly put, sometime around 1972, the testing field was co-opted by technocrats and process enthusiasts. Their passions were honorable, but those passions tended to marginalize the systemic, social, and psychological aspects of testing. (You might say those are "the icky parts.")

Sure, there was a lot of testing going on in the sixties, but the testing field had not yet defined itself, as such. The testing literature of the time described the activity as part of programming. In the IFIPS conference proceedings of the mid-sixties, rarely are dedicated testers or testing teams mentioned. Testing was often not distinguished from debugging. It was not until 1972 that the first book dedicated to testing was published: *Program Test Methods,* edited by Bill Hetzel. The book is essentially the proceedings of the Computer Program Test Methods Symposium held at the University of North Carolina at Chapel Hill.

As I analyze it, the Chapel Hill approach pursued two threads of development to make testing more reliable and manageable:

> 1. The technocratic thread: Develop tools and techniques to systematically and reliably discover certain kinds of defects (based on certain assumptions about the availability of complete specifications, sufficient time, sufficient tester skill and knowledge, source code, competent management, teams of people who follow methodical rules of behavior, and a product that is not too complex).

> 2. The process-control thread: Develop procedures and documents that humans would follow to discover certain defects reliably (based on similar assumptions as above).

And lo! Testing would enter its overproduced disco phase without ever having had its Summer of Love. Almost every testing book and academic testing paper since Hetzel has taken the same basic techno-procedural approach expressed in *Program Test Methods.* Except for a handful of anachronisms (such as the omission of brand-name test tools), the material in Hetzel's compilation would not raise eyebrows in the popular testing conferences today. That's how far we *haven't* come as a field.

The prime assumption behind the two threads is that testing is an ordinary technical problem. This assumption is invalid. And not just a little invalid. Especially in retrospect, it's clear that most of the testing problem (the social and the learning aspects of it) was ignored in order to make the remaining bit seem tractable. What we now know is that we can indeed find certain kinds of bugs reliably using formulaic techniques and tools, but many, many other kinds of bugs cannot be found or prevented that way. We also know that writing detailed test procedures doesn't scale. It's too slow and expensive, and scripted testing simply doesn't find many bugs.

Even at the time, Hetzel and others acknowledged that they were making a leap of faith.

Consider these snippets from the section written by Hetzel called Principles of Computer Program Testing:

"First we consider the problem of testable specifications. The common practice now is of course to leave much to implicit understanding. The resulting problems are well known. Ambiguity and misunderstanding are the cause of almost as many errors as logical coding. . . . Ideally, we would like the setting of the specifications to be independent of the testing process. In actual practice, the specification set is continually refined throughout program development and testing. Such feedback is simply forced by the imperfection of written specification methods."[2]

Notice that Hetzel saw the problem, but interpreted it as one of specification methodology.

But what if the people involved don't know what they want at the start of a complex project? What if they just don't understand the implications of what they want? If that's the case, then better specification methods won't help. Instead, testing needs to be an open-ended investigative process. The purpose of such testing is to help people who have varying desires and perspectives come to a better understanding of what the product is and what it should be.

Never mind that. Improving specification methods seems pretty doable to Hetzel:

> "It seems inevitable to me that reliable software will demand automatic examination. This in turn means unambiguous testable specification languages must evolve to allow descriptions about program behavior and the environments in which they operate."[3]

But he's not sure. . . .

> "Unambiguous specification languages and new logical reduction schemes which might make the goal of practical exhaustive testing a reality are far from available. In general, the methodology, techniques, and theory of system testing are entirely inadequate."[4]

Thirty-six years later, unambiguous specifications languages *are* available. Almost nobody uses them. Pick up the nearest specification, and you are likely to find it badly written and out-of-date. In fact, the Agile development trend has aggressively moved *away* from detailed and unambiguous specifications. Yet, the Chapel Hill attitude is still being touted in large organizations, still consuming enormous resources, and still falling far short of the promise.

For testing to progress as a discipline, it must first acknowledge and address the fundamental problem of testing: How can we observe, interact with, and learn about an arbitrarily complex and volatile artifact of technology—created by people who didn't fully understand what they were doing, created for people we may never meet, that may be used in places and in ways we may not anticipate—so as to learn about important problems it may have before it's too late and without driving our company out of business in the process?

Let me come back to Jerry. As I was reading Hetzel's book, clucking to myself, I stumbled across an unexpected passage contained in a section written by Fred Gruenberger. He criticizes the poor quality of testing advice given in programming textbooks, and then adds, "I have found only one text treatment that merits endorsement: the section of 'Preliminary Testing' in Leed's and Weinberg's *Computer Programming Fundamentals*."[5]

It turns out that Jerry wrote about testing in 1961! He wrote about it as an intellectually active process. "The testing of a

17

program, properly approached, is by far the most intriguing part of programming. Truly, the mettle of the programmer is tested along with the program. No puzzle addict could experience miraculous intricacies and subtleties of the trail left by a program gone wrong. . . . Testing out a program is seldom a step-by-step procedure. We normally must circle around, repeating ourselves, encompassing more of the total program each time we make a pass through it."[6] This passage anticipates what would come to be called exploratory testing, many years later. Notice how this passage focuses on the tester, not testing artifacts or tools. That's an unbroken thread throughout Jerry's work.

He also provided a simple, compelling heuristic for test design—"Test the normals, test the extremes, test the exceptions"—along with a vivid example of what happened on a bank software project where that guideline was not applied.

Jerry has been serious about testing for a long, long time. He was one of the earliest advocates of independent software testing teams. In 1961, when IBM held the Bald Peak Conference to discuss software development methodology, some 400 programmers were invited. At the time, that represented most of the programmers in the world. Jerry's group was the only one at that conference with a dedicated test team. (Bald Peak was also the event that introduced the notorious term "beta" into the lexicon of software development.)

Once I looked into it, I found other early works of Jerry's that show his way of thinking. Three of these publications, all developed during the 1960s, depict what testing can be, how to think about it, and how it might be studied. As I describe below, the assumptions and approach he takes with them are radically different from those of the Chapel Hill Symposium.

An Introduction to General Systems Thinking

An Introduction to General Systems Thinking was a long time in the writing. It developed out of problem-solving classes Jerry taught in the sixties.

Jerry calls *general systems thinking* the science of simplification. It is concerned with the study of complex, open systems in general, rather than with any specific system. The aim of general systems thinking is to help us understand the general relationships between systems and our simplified models of them, so that we can better observe, learn about, interact with, and build specific systems.

This is exactly what testers do! This is the critical element of test design. Unlike the Chapel Hill approach, which simplified the testing problem (essentially by defining all the hard parts of testing, such as learning what matters and what doesn't, as someone else's job), Jerry's idea was to teach people how to approach an arbitrarily complex situation without fear and to be a part of the simplification process. There is very little mention in the Chapel Hill material of how to think about an open-ended testing situation or how to develop skills as a tester. Jerry deals directly with those problems.

General systems thinking is essentially the logic of software testing. Jerry uses a running example, in the book, of three different people trying to analyze and describe a mysterious invention. I consider *An Introduction to General Systems Thinking* the first true textbook on the foundational skills of testing. Still, it is virtually unknown by the heirs of Chapel Hill.

Experiments in Problem Solving, **Ph.D. dissertation, 1965**

Unlike almost all the other famous names in software testing, Jerry earned his Ph.D. in the field of psychology. Jerry studied how people solve problems. His research involved what I would call a problem in exploratory testing. He showed his subjects a running program, and they had to predict how it would behave. Jerry approached the problem like a good social scientist, embracing the complexity and subtleties of the situation:

> "There is no way to be certain that all subjects share the experimenter's view of what the problem is, and the more complex the problem we are dealing with, the less chance there is of anything being shared among the subjects. Why not give up the futile attempts to force the subjects into a Procrustean bed and design experiments which measure their differences, not conceal them? To take this approach, we must

abandon the idea of measuring 'success,' at least in any fixed way, because each of the subjects—having a different view of what the task is—is working toward a different measure of success."[7]

He approached his research as an exploratory study, but the precision and richness of his measurements allowed for rigorous analysis, too:

"One of the frightening things about the richness of this set of experiments is the way new insights keep turning up each time the 10,000 or so bits of each experiment are recombined in some new manner. How many times in the history of science have discoveries been left hidden for want of the right point of view, as when Uranus appeared on the photographs of several astronomers before its 'discovery'?"[8]

Jerry's research, completed the year before I was born, continues to inform the development, in my own community, of experiments and experiential learning exercises that help us develop better testers and better heuristics for testers.

"Natural Selection as Applied to Computers and Programs," 1970

In this paper,[9] originally written in 1967, Jerry shows how a program can be viewed as an adaptive system that is bound by the dynamics of Darwin's great hypothesis. The upshot of this, in modern terms, is a criticism of scripted regression testing. Jerry warns that when a system that continues to change or that is in a changing environment is subjected to a fixed set of tests, it will inevitably over-adapt to those tests, leading to a higher probability of severe and surprising failures in the field. This will happen, regardless of how good those tests are when first designed.

Jerry presents testing, in this paper, as a dynamic pursuit rather than a problem of producing a set of fixed artifacts.

20

The Father of Software Testing

When I started researching this piece, I intended to set out my case for why Jerry Weinberg should be considered the father of software testing. My reading convinced me that he's *not* the father of what most people know *today* as software testing. You might say that the testing baby was stolen at Chapel Hill. Rather, along with a few others—such as physicist Richard Feynman and philosophers David Hume, Sextus Empiricus, and Socrates—I would call Jerry Weinberg a prince of testers.

Though it may take many years and a revolution in our educational system, I believe his approach will someday dominate the field. It deserves to, because it works. I'm talking about his experiential methods of teaching, his insistence on dealing with the world in all its complexity, and his application of psychology to technical projects.

Before closing, I can't resist sharing a final quote from one of Jerry's papers. It describes an experiment in which two instructors attempt to demonstrate by example what their students believed was impossible:

> "[This paper] is about the way people write programs, and teach others to write programs. We believe that programming is a practical subject, not a mathematical one, and must be taught by instructors who are prepared to demonstrate how the principles they espouse may be put into action. We believe that 'structured programming' does not mean some rigid set of mathematical rules imposed on programmers, but an attitude about programming that says you can always improve if you only examine the way you currently do things. If, through exercises such as these, frankly discussed with our students, we can make them program self-consciously, we shall have succeeded as teachers."[10]

Jerry has done the same with testing. In so doing, he has inspired me and many others to continue his work.

3

It's All Relative

Michael Bolton

I'm not sure when I first heard Jerry Weinberg say, "Compared to what?"

It may have been at our first meeting. A bunch of people were at the table, the night before the official opening of the 2002 AYE Conference. The dinner plates had been pushed aside, people were licking their spoons after dessert, and the long evening conversation had begun. At one point, the subject was languages, or Japan, and I idly remarked that Japanese was considered hard to learn. Jerry peered over his glasses and said, "Most Japanese kids learn it before they hit kindergarten." (Maybe he said "Compared to what?" just before he said that.)

Or maybe it was a few days later, sitting in a circle during an AYE session. Someone commented that software development was expensive. "Compared to what?" asked Jerry.

Maybe it was in another session, when Jerry recounted working, many years earlier, on a program that incorporated a part number. He had asked the client if there were any special characters that the program had to handle. "None," said the client.

The program crashed on the first character of the first part number that it tried to process—a pound symbol. Dismayed, Jerry went with printout in hand to the customer. "I thought you said there were no special characters!"

"There's nothing special about *that*," said the customer. "There's one of those on *every* part number."

Back in the AYE session, Jerry emphasized the point: "'Special' compared to what?"

Maybe it was in yet another AYE workshop, when someone asked for the best solution to some problem. You can guess what

Jerry asked in reply. I realized that he was repeatedly asking that simple and elegant question "compared to what?" that most of us don't ask often enough. Yet if we asked it consistently, considered a variety of comparisons, and provided a number of possible answers, we'd be more precise in what we were asking for, and more likely to get what we wanted. "'Best' compared to what?" is a question that we can apply helpfully to the notion of "best practices," and that idea formed the basis for the one of my first published articles.

Through Jerry's books, I had been aware of his definition of quality as "value to some person." There's a wealth of wisdom in that definition: that different people value different things in different ways. That is, quality is value compared *by whom?* Could quality itself be subjective? A little further reading revealed Jerry's definition of value—what someone will do (or pay) to have his or her requirements met.[11] Someone? More subjectivity?

All this was a little nerve-racking at first. It removed the comfortable security that other ideas about quality had provided me—"the absence of defects," "conformance to requirements," "fitness for use," and so on. Later, I realized that these definitions were just as subjective, as soon as one added the words that, on reflection, were manifestly missing: "according to some person." I had been using these subjective definitions for a long time, believing—along with most other people—that they were objective. Once I recognized this error, a large number of puzzling situations stopped being so puzzling. The confusion was beginning to clear, but slowly.

Several years later, the editor of our local software testing association journal asked a number of experts for their definitions of software quality. Jerry's reply seemed a little cranky. It was:

> "I'll stick with the definition that I gave in my *Quality Software Management* series: 'Quality is value to some person or persons.' What's the fuss? This definition is pragmatic and has held up well for fifty years. Why change? Or do you still think quality is some objective measurement, something in the software rather than in its relationship to the people who use it, pay for it, or are victimized by it?"[12]

Around the same time, I was looking through *An Introduction to General Systems Thinking,* a book that bears repeated browsing and re-reading. In one of my excursions, I noticed that Jerry identified "purpose" in the same way—as a relationship between the person and the thing. Having seen two instances of this pattern, I was on the lookout for others.

One of the early ones for me was the one-word tautology: *obvious.* Obviousness is clearly a relationship between a person and a concept. In high school, we had a very opaque mathematics teacher who would leave most of the class behind, introducing a daunting new concept as "intuitively obvious." Even as teenagers, we snickered at the teacher because we recognized the tautology: Something is obvious for someone to whom it is obvious, and not obvious for someone to whom it is not obvious. Obviousness is based on your relationship with an old concept and your perceptions of what's new. Obviously.

Another relationship word is "rational," which Jerry highlighted on SHAPE, early in my years of participation in that forum. One of the participants complained about his coworkers, writing that he "just can't think of rational reasons why these things are done." Jerry replied,

> "That's because you haven't developed your irrational mind. 90 percent-plus of what people do is not rational—at least not based on the same set of presuppositions that you (or I) use. It would be rational to learn how to live with so much irrationality around you.
>
> Software maintainers definitely have to learn to deal with 'irrationality,' and the first step in that learning is to stop calling it irrationality. Call it 'rational from the point of view of another set of values.'"[13]

Or, as McLuhan and Nevin maintain, psychologists report that madmen are rigorously logical, but their premises are irrelevant.[14]

Following a habit suggested by Jerry, among others, I decided to write in my notebook a list of words that might seem absolute, but that are in fact relative. The list got long quickly:

complexity, test cases, bug counts, bugs(!), tests(!), problems, match, correctness, productivity, jargon, euphemism, ambiguity, intuitive, boundary, equivalence, responsiveness, randomness, target, victim, context, space, done, system, structure, and so on.

It went, and it goes, on and on. I pondered what I had learned so far, and came up with a modest attempt at a general systems law, which I call The Relative Rule:

A description of something intangible as "X" really means "X *to some person, at some time.*"

Or, as it might appear in *An Introduction to General Systems Thinking,*

$f(x) = f(person, time,...)$

So, if X is merely X to some person at some time, it can be seen or understood differently (by some other person, or by the same person) at some other time. This means that many things are likely to be subjective and ambiguous.

When a developer says that he's "done" coding, he means that according to some set of heuristics, he believes that the code works. When he says that it "works," he means it appears to fulfill some requirement, to some degree, in some set of circumstances. Or as Jerry himself said once, again in the SHAPE forum:

> "When you hear someone say, 'It works,' immediately translate that into, 'We haven't tried very hard to make it fail, and we haven't been running it very long or under very diverse conditions, but so far we haven't seen any failures, though we haven't been looking too closely, either.'"

For as long as I've been working with software development—as a programmer, a support person, a tester, a program manager—I've been hearing that subjectivity, ambiguity, and uncertainty are the greatest threats to effective work. But of course, "subjectivity," "ambiguity," "uncertainty," and "threat" are also relationships between some person and the thing being observed—they're

THE GIFT OF TIME

perceptions, wherein there may be an advantage. If we follow the heuristic that perception is reality, something that can be perceived differently *is* different and can therefore be approached differently. We can broaden our perceptions by broadening our conceptions. They don't have to impose limitations on each other, and we can escape the prisons we choose to live inside.[15]

Thus, instead of being a problem, ambiguity can help us solve problems. After all, a problem is "an undesirable situation that is significant to and may be solvable by some agent, although probably with some difficulty."[16] That is, "problem" follows The Relative Rule:

A problem is a problem to some person, at some time.

And a corollary:

A problem might be no problem to some other person, at some other time.

At the session of PSL that I attended, one participant described the difficulty her group had with a particular exercise: "The complexity of the problem screwed us up." Jerry pointed out the relationship: "Your reaction to the complexity of the problem screwed you up."

In the face of a complex problem, our fear of uncertainty causes us to seek out simple outcomes, and that fear can freeze us. But complexity isn't an attribute; it's a relationship between the observer and the observed. Change the relationship, and we change the problem.

Recalling that a problem is a function of time, we could choose to change the time dimension. Perhaps the problem will go away, or perhaps a solution will reveal itself. Malcolm Gladwell, an author and systems thinker, focuses on rapid cognition in his book *Blink*.[17] He suggests that we can sometimes improve the quality of our judgments by removing information and making faster decisions, simpler observations, and more-rapid assessments. Since problems are problems for some person, we could also choose to involve some person who has the requisite skill or observational capacity to recognize the way out.

Or maybe we could change our own relationship with problems and complexity, embracing them rather than rejecting them. Something might seem complex, defying our attempts to simplify it with our limited observations. But what if we take a little risk and *add* complexity, temporarily, by choosing to make other observations? We then have a richer set of observations from which we can choose, paying attention to some, rejecting or ignoring others. By alternating between the simple and the complex, we can get traction on a problem. Different observations point down different paths of comparison and contrast, where the relationships might be more comprehensible. The general systems approach—which allows us to model and recognize patterns of behavior, problems, and solutions across disciplines—yields insight into the discipline in which we're currently involved. Ontogeny doesn't recapitulate phylogeny, but oncology might recapitulate psychology.

Yet another approach might be to choose to become a different person. The most active, most lively, and most powerful minds that I can think of—Leonardo, Richard Feynman, Herbert Simon, and, yes, Jerry Weinberg—have taken this approach, constantly studying new disciplines and absorbing new ways of looking at the world. G.F. Smith called this the concept of requisite variety: "Complicate yourself if you want to understand complicated environments."[18]

Jonathan Miller is such a complicated fellow—a writer, broadcaster, medical doctor, comedian, and director of stage, television, and opera. He was one of the members of *Beyond the Fringe,* a stage show that has had a profound influence on British comedy from the early 1960s through the present day. He once presented a lecture at the Ontario Science Centre entitled "Humour and Science," in which he presented a scientific perspective on why humor exists in all human cultures. He postulated that since humor is so universal, there must be a corresponding biological payoff, an evolutionary advantage. The advantage that humor confers, he suggested, is that it allows us to alter our categories—to recognize that things can be different.

Altering categories and exploiting the relative nature of things is a comedian's standard practice. Consider this joke by Steven Wright—a total stranger told it to me, a little while back, quite consistent with Wright's storytelling style:

> A guy came up to me the other day and said, "Your socks don't match." I said, "Yes they do. I go by thickness."

Here's one that could be told about bald-headed Canadian men in their mid forties, but I heard it this way . . . from a blond:

> A blond is walking along a riverbank, seeking to cross. She sees no tunnel, no bridge, but eventually she does see another blond across the way. She calls out, "How do you get to the other side?" After a long pause, the answer comes back: "You're *on* the other side."

These seemingly insignificant jokes reveal important concepts in general systems theory. The recognition of relativity and uncertainty were the keys to some of the greatest discoveries in mathematics and physics. Physics is about the relationship of a body to space, but space itself can be described as a relationship between two bodies. Copernicus, Galileo, and Newton realized that extremely complex problems in celestial mechanics could be solved when we change our perspective to put something other than ourselves and our planet at the center of the problem. Einstein extended this idea when, through general relativity, he revealed that time itself isn't absolute; it is relative to the person making the observation. After Russell and Whitehead released *Principia Mathematica*, which they expected to be the last word in mathematics, Gödel quickly determined that there wasn't a last word, and there wouldn't be; any notational system is either inconsistent or incomplete. Mathematics and physics, traditionally regarded as bastions of certainty, turn out to be subjective, uncertain, and heuristic.

Music is about relationships: the pitches of different notes; one instrument and another; the position of notes in relation to time. There is a constant interplay of each new note as figure, relating to the ground of the notes that have appeared before it. Music depends on suspense, uncertainty, and surprise for its richness. Most importantly, music is about the figure of the sound in relationship to the ground of silence. Listen to any piece of music scored for an ensemble, and follow a single instrument. You'll notice that there are often rests, gaps in which that instrument is not playing—these add a rich dynamic to the music; the holes are greater than some of the parts.

James Bach recently pointed me to a book called *Discussion of the Method*,[19] by Billy Vaughn Koen, in which Koen seeks to articulate the universal problem-solving method. Koen, an engineer, starts with the engineering problem-solving method. Engineers attempt to come up with the best possible solution for the moment, given their own knowledge, the available resources, and the given constraints. Koen points out that the field of engineering, the engineer's organization, and the engineer herself all have different, overlapping, and constantly changing sets of knowledge, resources, and constraints. Solving an engineering problem depends on the state of the art for all three of the engineer, her organization, and the field. Engineering solutions are context-dependent, which means that we can't point to a solution and label it "best," except in a given context. Even then, we can't be sure that some better solution wasn't right under our nose; our nose may be in the way of our eyes. Since no solution can be guaranteed perfect, the best we can do is to use heuristics—fallible methods, conducive to learning, for solving a problem or making a decision. Nothing is certain—even the statement that everything is heuristic.[20]

I used to wonder how we could comprehend and deal with a world in which nothing is certain and everything is subjective. That's easier now that I realize where Jerry—and the people he has influenced, especially James Bach—have been taking me. The knowledge that things can be different is the fundamental insight of my profession, testing.[21] Our clients depend on us to find out how our products relate to the systems in which they participate and to the people who use them. To do that effectively, we must explore other dimensions of what people might mean by simple statements and how the system might react when we change some condition or assumption. If we wish to be effective when we test the ability of a program to save a file, we must think about the ways in which the system is constructed, the steps involved in the process, the information being saved, how people accomplish the task, the circumstances in which the action happens, and the timing of all of the above. It would be impossible to list all possible conditions, circumstances, and expectations; instead, we have to examine those things heuristically and incompletely, in the ways that might matter most to our clients and how they relate to the task.

When James and I teach, we give a modeling exercise in which we ask students to identify the dimensions relevant to testing a common object—a wine glass. Part of the exercise is to encourage students to question the mission by asking what "dimensions," "identify," "relevant," and "testing" mean, since each one of these words contains the trap of a dangling comparison. As part of the exercise, we're perfectly willing to explain what we mean, if someone asks. When we say "dimensions," we mean any factor that could vary from glass to glass, or in one glass over time; by "relevant to testing," we mean a factor that may be of interest to some real or imagined client.

I consistently find it remarkable how few people question their mission and thereby fall into the trap, but what's even more remarkable is the poverty of the models that result from failing, implicitly or explicitly, to take a more expansive view. For example, I once gave the wine glass exercise to a programmer, and he filled a page of my notebook with dimensions—yet each was a physical dimension of the glass. When I pointed out to him that these were all physical dimensions, he said, "Yes, so they are. I'm getting to the other ones"—whereupon he filled another page with physical dimensions. Yet, the object of testing the wine glass is not to determine its relationships to rulers and calipers and scales of various kinds, but its purpose, its value, its history, its contents, and its relationship to other wine glasses. Those are all relationships to its users—and to the people who want to understand those relationships.

Understanding relationships and embracing complexity allows us to escape Testing Flatland and to explore other dimensions in the greater space. In *Take Today,* McLuhan notes that the method of exploration,

> ". . . begins by the admission of ignorance and difficulties. Such a statement will tend to be a tentative groping. The blind man's cane picks up the relation of things in his environment by the quality of resonance.

His tapping tells him what objects are adjacent to his stick. If his stick were connected to any of these objects, he would be helpless so far as orientation was concerned. This is always the plight of the logical method. It is useless for exploration. Its very strength makes it irrelevant."

McLuhan, a professor of English literature, was as much of a systems thinker as any hard scientist. That's not surprising, because literature evolved from storytelling, which was the principal human means of making sense of the world. This business of relating things to one another has been going on for a long time. Associative language—simile and metaphor—used to be the way that we remembered things, before we attempted to capture and freeze them with writing. People remembered the relationships between the constellations by associating them with stories about the gods, which in turn allowed them to explain natural phenomena.

Imprecision became a more serious problem in our recent history, when we began to use tools to help in solving our problems. Computing machines—very fast, but breathtakingly stupid—depend on us to express both the task and the data to a painfully precise degree. Scientific precision, specialization, and technologies like writing have allowed us to make considerable progress, but lately, it seems to me, we've been focusing too much on attempting to make the imprecision problem disappear for the purpose of serving our tools. As long as humans are involved, ambiguity and subjectivity are not only inevitable but necessary if we're going to make progress.

That's because imagination depends on simile and metaphor—those figures of speech that allow us to describe things we've never seen in terms of things we have seen. Each person sees different sets of relationships between two things. We might choose to view subjectivity as a problem, and then try to ignore or deny it—or instead, we could view the relative nature of things as a path toward recognizing and appreciating a richer, more human world.

4

When a Therapist Meets an IT Community

Jean McLendon
Interviewed by Sherry Heinze

Jean, you've known Jerry for many years. Can you tell me how you met?

I first remember Jerry from Virginia Satir's Process Community, in Crested Butte, in 1986. There were about ninety people in the group. Jerry and his wife, Dani, were sitting to Virginia's right, and I was sitting to Virginia's left. I remember that Jerry would often share during Temperature Readings. He would share something he had written, or a thought, or a question. That was when I first noticed him.

What were your first impressions of the Weinbergs?

Jerry was large and vocal; he took a lot of notes and seemed to be a highly conscientious student. He was strikingly intent on not missing even a tiny gem from Virginia. He was casually dressed and appeared to be very approachable. Jerry was so engaged as a student that I was not attracted to him in a social way. Dani was quieter and more mysterious. She was obviously engaged and interested, but in the lingo of anthropology, she never "went native." However deeply she valued the Satir Growth Model and regarded Virginia, her passions would eventually lead her to working with dogs and their families. Some years later, though, in a phone conversation, Dani was talking about a young couple who had brought a dog to her for obedience training. Dani talked about the couple, the dog, and her sense of what was going on between

32

and among the cast of characters. We could only laugh when we simultaneously recognized she was in fact doing excellent family therapy. Jerry and I have continued on with our commitment to share Satir with the world in a more traditional manner.

I knew from the beginning that Jerry and Dani weren't therapists. I don't remember how I knew. At that time, 80 percent, or more, of the Process Community were therapists or human service workers. I had no real contact with Jerry and Dani. We were not in the same small group. I was not in any exercises with either of them.

Jerry's connection was to Virginia and the Satir model, not to the Community. Because they were a couple, Dani and Jerry made a full circle with learning Satir. Jerry sent me something some years ago where he took notes about Crested Butte and noticed that the trainers had a special look and wondered if he would have it too after some time.

In a sense, Jerry was a foreigner coming in. He came after reading *Peoplemaking*.[22] He came with eyes wide open, ears open, an eager beaver to get what he could, very focused.

How did you come to work with them?

Virginia became critically ill in 1988. I had planned to take the summer off from training and travel to Europe with my partner. I received a call from the Avanta president, Marilyn Peers, saying that Virginia needed me to go to Crested Butte and direct the Process Community. I talked to my partner, who agreed that I should go. I called Virginia and offered to go to California—which is where she was living—and to take care of her. Virginia said no; she needed me at Crested Butte. So, I went to Colorado instead of Europe.

I asked Virginia for consultation with the Process Community. Virginia said, "Of course," but she quickly and understandably became very focused on her illness. I sent her a video tape of the first session. She said it was great. We had no other contact about the Process Community.

Jerry and Dani had bought a place in Crested Butte. They became part of my support system. It was not an easy year. My "sibling trainers" in the Process Community were upset about

Virginia, and upset that I had been designated acting director. Jerry started putting information into his computer to be used as handouts. That was a tremendous help to me. As the Process Community took shape, it became easier. Diana Hall was there, and she helped, too.

How did you go from there to create the first Congruent Leadership Change Shop?

After a couple of summer intensive trainings with Virginia, Dani and Jerry offered to help Virginia bring her teachings to the business world. They imagined cocreating a new residential intensive leadership program, one that would build on their Problem Solving Leadership workshop. Virginia was willing, pleased, and appreciative of their offer. This was planned before Virginia became ill. During the summer of 1988, when they again connected with the annual Process Community Training Institute, they were to begin planning what would become the Change Shop, the seven-day Congruent Leadership Development workshop.

Rochelle Ford, Avanta's administrator, was at Crested Butte for a while during the Process Community in 1988. About midway through the training, she told me that Virginia very much wanted me to work with Jerry and Dani on the leadership program since she could not.

Jerry and Dani had to have been very disappointed that Virginia was not there. I don't know how they got word that Virginia wanted them to move forward with me in her absence. I believe, however, that we each had our reservations, apprehensions, and excitements—yet regardless of Virginia's condition, which we came to understand was terminal, we were committed to sharing Satir with the world.

Dani, Jerry, and I were basically an arranged triad, or a strange breed of a merger. We knew we could always say, "this doesn't fit," but we wanted to give the potential alliance a try. Our first meeting sold me on our ability to work together. Unlike other business partnerships where I gravitated to people whom I have strong relationships with, in this case, it was partnering with people who shared a dream. The first item of business was to determine if we wanted to partner. My answer bubbled up energetically in me when one of us suggested we figure out a way to work together to check out how well we might do as a working triad. It was not difficult for us to find a volunteer who was open to getting consultation from our budding triad. Diana Hall was dealing with some complexities, so we offered to see if we could be helpful. We spent an afternoon working with her and decided we would proceed. As I reflect on how quickly I realized that I was up for the adventure, I recall the relief I felt when we decided not just to talk about how it might be but actually to have an experiential pretest. The evidence of their commitment to learn via here-and-now experience was compelling. My own self-esteem issues about working with the Weinbergs and their people (in other words, computer people), had me wondering if I would fit in, be smart enough, or feel like a fish out of water. I knew I could teach Satir experientially, though, and now I knew that we could dance together with a client. We shared a STAR (in Satir terms, a client or identified patient) and created a warm and encouraging way for her to move forward with more vision and focus.

We gathered that fall at their home in Nebraska and began serious planning for our inaugural leadership workshop for change artists. We spent about four days creating a design and deciding who would do what. Jerry took on the biggest part, creating the handouts and doing the marketing, with Lois French's help. Dani focused on finding students in Europe and Canada.

We surely had our differences and early on realized that we each had different long suits. At some point, we gave labels to each of our strengths. Jerry was the primo problem-solver, Dani was the teacher, and I was the therapist. Though there was blurring of these roles over time, we remained fairly true to our roots.

One thing—the really unique characteristic in Change Shop—was the point at which the participants became responsible for designing their own learning. It was Jerry's idea. I thought it was brilliant. It was a powerful foreign element both for individual members and as a collective. It was a huge opportunity to appreciate their unique ways of handling stress.

How did Change Shop evolve over time?

The first year, I did 80 percent of the Satir demos and the Satir work. As Jerry and Dani became more experienced in doing the experiential and personal work, they did more of it. By the end, it was just Jerry and me, and we did about 50 percent each. I don't remember if it was Jerry or Dani who named it the Congruent Leadership Change Shop. The name was right on target. We wanted to create artists who would be effective leaders of positive change.

As Dani's interest and success in dog obedience training grew, we began to lose her. Jerry and I remained interested, and had the juice to keep going. Dani was supportive of our continuing. Our team MO was that we each had our specific presentation pieces. It was fairly easy for us to pick up Dani's pieces, but her unique spin and essence was a loss.

The people who came to Change Shop had been through Problem Solving Leadership first. I went to PSL once. It was a good program, but I decided not to become involved.

My colleagueship and friendship remains, now after twenty years. For me, I have been gifted many times over by my association with the Weinbergs and my dear friends and colleagues in the IT community. This community in many ways reflected what I saw in Jerry when he entered his first Process Community. This community has an ongoing love affair with learning. These people are eager to see how they can improve their functioning. They are oriented to an honest reflection of the facts and of their observations. They have a freshness about what I call the "universality of emotionality." They are not taken with pretense or formalities. They own their limitations but are not stymied by them. They are courageous in their willingness to go beyond what is familiar. Their minds are quick, and if they trust you, their hearts warm quickly. They don't overdrink. They are respectful of boundaries. They know how to express gratitude and appreciation. They are often brilliant and know that the quality of the code they write and the programs they design are dependent on the quality of the connection they have with the end user. When they think of their work being *friendly*, they mean that it makes sense, works predictably, and helps us not to waste time or feel stupid, dismissed, ignored, or regretful to have purchased their product. Business owners who want the best from their computer-savvy employees need to recognize that they have, built into most IT professionals, a sales/marketing/service/customer-relations person, all in one. They want their products to be bug free; they want their customers to be satisfied; and they know that haste makes waste.

Can you tell me something about how the Change Shop program worked?

We decided on the content when we met in Nebraska. When I had used Satir in organizations previously, I had to slide it in. I used Blake and Mouton's[23] work on leadership style and the Myers-Briggs Type Indicator,[24] then overlaid them with Satir. We decided to go directly to Satir with no attempt to reframe or dilute it for the Change Shop. That made it a more exciting commitment, to me. We used the Satir system for all it was worth. The material was not dampened down because the students weren't therapists. We started for years with a very emotional piece on the Five Freedoms. We dove into deep water from the beginning. After a while, we began to feel very confident with each other, so we could continue to innovate.

Jerry liked to teach from stories. Sometimes, he would get carried away. Dani and I tried to get him to tighten up, which he did, once he started doing more of the experiential work. Jerry's stories helped people ground their learnings for applicability.

No matter how difficult a workshop was, at the end, I always felt it was worth the effort: to see people opening up, and to see their personal learning and how they could use the model.

Did you do other work together?

Jerry and I wrote an article for IEEE together. Writing has not been something that comes easily to me. Jerry was very supportive and has always offered to help. His ability to write, his knowledge and sources, allow him to just slide pieces in and as they fit. Jerry made the project very easy for me.

We had a colleague in common in New Orleans whom I had worked with previously. Our colleague wanted to bring in couples for training and include leadership training. It was a different culture, people who had done a lot of therapy. We only did it once.

Do you see advantages in working with mixed groups of business-people, therapists, and academics rather than groups with similar backgrounds?

My preference is to work with a mixed group. Often, therapists' training exposes them to the territory of personal development through experiential learning. For many in business, this is a new territory. Because it is new, there is a freshness. They are not jaded, not deluded, and they don't need to prove their competence. In that sense, they are more open. Businesspeople ask questions that the therapists like hearing the answers to, but would not think to ask. This provides a foundation for clarifying assumptions. Not having been in the territory, businesspeople have no idea of how they are supposed to respond or be. That kind of authenticity is refreshing. They need to understand what it is about before taking a dive. Things need to make sense to them. That expands the meaning for everybody.

Did working with Jerry and other IT folks change your practice, or help it grow in ways that would not otherwise have happened?

It really gave me an opportunity to see very clearly the relevance of Satir work for people in business. I had previously worked with governmental and nonprofit organizations. IT was a stretch for me. When I began the yearlong program, it was just therapists. People from Change Shop asked for more training. I invited them in. Therapists are accustomed to being trained with other thera-pists. One student objected to having businesspeople in the program. I told her why I thought it would enrich the program. She came back again the next year. Including IT people with their questions and observational skills helped everyone. If I had not done Change Shop, I would probably just have trained therapists. I got it that the Satir model was for human systems, any human system.

I was never sure early on if I wanted to work doing therapy or training and consultation. I vacillated between them. I still do. The work with businesspeople was very validating about the model. It has kept me and my practice fresh to work with different people from different backgrounds and settings. It is very affirming. It gives me confidence about the universals, about how much more we have in common than different. I have a special enjoyment when IT people come to me for therapy. I know something about them because I know the culture. I have an appreciative, positive stereotype. I assume they will speak the truth. One time, I asked a patient what he was feeling, and he said he was frustrated and bored. I believe there are a lot of people who would not tell me if they were bored.

How does that influence what you do now and who you are now?

I have taken very seriously the need for the larger Satir community to be enriched by this community. As past president of the Virginia Satir Global Network, I am very pleased that two members of our current board come from this community. This organization, formerly called Avanta, began with a huge mission and a membership of primarily therapists. When I reentered the community a few years ago and became president, it made no sense to me that we were a group of therapists. We needed businesspeople and others who worked in different contexts. Basically, we just needed to open the doors to whoever else was interested in learning and sharing the teachings of Satir. Virginia used to talk about the day when we would have satellites and be able to talk across the globe. I knew Avanta would need more skills. I could not imagine not having people like those I came to know in Jerry's community. I think this will be one of my biggest contributions to the larger Satir network.

Is there anything I've missed?

My admiration for Jerry and Dani's commitment to their community. Satir is a pathway into skills for being more fully human. They have shared this pathway with courage and great generosity. I don't know of anyone else who has carried what was a family therapy approach forward into business like Jerry has. He has had a huge impact on the lives of people across many businesses and countries. There are many people across our world who are grateful to him for the changes they have been able to make in their lives. Jerry has been very therapeutic. I hope members of Jerry's community will continue to share Satir with the world. You do not have to be a therapist to be therapeutic.

Would you like to add anything?

I would like people to know that we had fun. Dani and Jerry and I used to drive together to the places where we gave workshops. I would fly into Albuquerque, and then we would drive to the workshop site. The trips were part of team-building and catching up. In Arizona, one time, there was a flood. We drove over a bridge that we couldn't have crossed two hours later. It was thrilling. We worked in places that offered activities for us and the participants. I remember horseback riding in the desert, swimming with Jerry, shopping with Dani, rug shopping on the way to Change Shop, and going out for nice lunches. We stayed in a condo one time, and all three of our Macs lived on our dining room table. When others were eating, we were laughing and moaning while doing our e-mail. I have lots of very warm and fun memories. We don't get together much these days, but when we do, our triad spark is very present.

5

Tool Time

Sue Petersen

I know a man who carries his brain on a string around his neck. It's not really his brain, of course, but the small nugget of turquoise does rather look like a brain. It's a touchstone—an icon—that reminds him to use his intellect as well as his heart when he's involved in a stressful situation at work. For the same reason, I wear my courage on my wrist, embodied in a Navajo-made sterling silver bracelet. When I'm upset, my throat closes up and I have a hard time getting out the words I need to say. But when I move my wrist and feel the weight of the silver, I can remind myself to take a deep breath, center myself physically, speak my truth quietly and calmly, and then deal with the consequences.

My bracelet and my friend's nugget are both tools. There's nothing magical about them, but they are unobtrusive and easy to customize and can be very useful in the struggles of daily life. The best managers I know have many different tools in their repertoire and are able to pick and choose among them, as the situation requires. Over the years, I've adapted some of the tools I've seen other people use, and I've created some of my own. Let's take a look at my tool tray.

Sterling Courage

I bought my first bracelet in 1996, in Santa Fe, New Mexico. I'd just finished the seven-day Change Shop workshop with Jerry Weinberg and Jean McLendon, and I had a free day before I caught my flight home. I spent most of the afternoon exploring the plaza in Santa Fe, browsing the works of the native artists who set up shop under the Palace of the Governors. Jerry had written about his "tool kit" in *More Secrets of Consulting,* and we'd spent much of the week looking at and using different parts of a suggested kit for managers and consultants. Jerry's kit includes the Yes/No Medallion (to remind yourself that you *do* have a choice), the Wishing Wand (to remind yourself that things *can* be better), and, of course, the Courage Stick (to help you conquer fear). I knew that I was looking for something that could function as my Courage Stick, since I thought it might be rather awkward for me to carry around a three-foot-long piece of mesquite wood at work every day.

Then I found a beautiful, very discreet and subtle bracelet with the story of a seven-day bear hunt stamped into the silver. To the Native Americans of the Southwest, the bear embodies courage and spirit and perseverance. *Perfect!* I wore that bracelet day and night for years, and it helped me handle some extremely stressful confrontations at work.

I still have that first Courage Bracelet, although I have collected several others that I match to the situation at hand, my mood, and my outfit. One of my favorites has a carved bear head on it; another reminds me of watching the stars at night with my youngest son. The one I'm wearing today has a corn stalk on it to represent the abundance of life that I sometimes forget to notice when I'm busy and distracted.

Programming a Survival Guide

Jerry talks a lot about survival rules (see *Becoming a Technical Leader)*, those subconscious rules of living that we all learn when we are very small and trying to get along in a confusing world. Jerry is very effective at helping people identify their rules and transform them into guides instead of ironclad no-exceptions-allowed laws. I take every opportunity I'm given to watch this process of transformation unfold in workshops and classes. I'm learning to identify and sometimes to transform my own rules, and the further along this path I get, the more effective I am as a manager and coach, and as a human being.

But I'm a bit of a contrarian, and I eventually started wondering about the mental processes behind survival rules. Could I learn to use the process itself for good instead of for evil? Oh, don't get me wrong, I don't want to create a race of mental zombies to serve my every need! ("Yes, Mistress," my zombie would say. "Next task, Mistress?") But there's obviously some pretty powerful mental hardwiring behind survival rules, and it would be nice to harness that design for something positive in my life today. Is it possible to create new survival rules? Well, let's not create rules, because we don't want to be trapped by them. But it would be nice to be able to create a guide or two that will kick in and shepherd us along a predetermined path when we're stressed out and about to blow.

The thought wasn't totally foreign to me. I'd read (and later practiced) something similar, way back in the 1980s, in the book Patricia Gail Burnham wrote about obedience-training her greyhounds.[25]

Sighthounds, such as greyhounds, can be particularly maddening to train. They're intelligent, but they're not particularly interested in pleasing you. Moreover, they can easily outrun you! Gail taught herself to "program" a particularly meaningful phrase before she lost her temper with a dog. The phrase had to be relevant to her relationship with that particular dog, and it had to be something she really cared about in that particular situation. But when those two criteria were met and she practiced the phrase beforehand, she could go from serious frustration and anger immediately into calm and effective problem-solving. Cool: A survival guide!

A survival guide should act like the high-temp cutoff on your water heater. In the old days, before such safety features were standard, it was not unknown for a water heater to overheat and go off like a bomb. I've heard of at least one heater located in a basement that went clear through the roof of a three-story house. Those things are *dangerous.* These days, when the high temp cutoff is triggered, the power shuts off so the heater cools down instead of exploding.

The important points about creating a working survival guide appear to be relevance and practice. The guide you are trying to create must be something that is *very important to you, in that situation.* And you must practice it beforehand—it's too much to expect yourself to magically pull it out of thin air, in the heat of battle. One of my favorite guides goes like this: "You can't punish him for something he doesn't understand." That little phrase saves me enormous stress and anger when things aren't going right with a horse or another animal. I care very much about being humane and effective with my animals, and it's not fair to expect them to think exactly like humans. And when my guide kicks in, I can toggle from hot anger to calm problem-solving. I may not be able to fix the problem immediately, but at least I won't make it worse. I can leave and try again later.

Whose Hula Hoop Is This, Anyway?

Not all survival guides are phrases. Some of mine are images in my head. I learned this one from my colleague Rick Brenner, when he demonstrated it for a group of us one day.

Stand in the middle of the room. Imagine that you are holding a child's hula hoop around your waist. (Most people of a certain vintage know what a hula hoop is. If you don't, imagine a thin plastic tube, bent into a circle about four feet in diameter, light-weight enough to swing around your waist and to manipulate easily. They're lots of fun to dance and to play with.) Now, imagine that everything within your hula hoop is *your* stuff, the people and projects and things that *you* are responsible for. You have both the authority and the responsibility that you need to take care of these things. Now, imagine that someone else walks into the room. Of course, they'll have their own hula hoop full of their own stuff. Unfortunately, sometimes their hula hoop over-laps yours. Maybe they dropped some of their stuff into your hula hoop when you weren't looking, or maybe you reached over and knowingly accepted it. Maybe they're part of your team and you're *supposed* to work together on this task. In any case, once you're hooked, you can't move without affecting them, and every move they make tugs and yanks on you. It's very difficult to stay balanced and effective under these circumstances. Even if you do manage to get things done, fighting their tugs can take a terrible toll on your time and energy. And, of course, they're almost certainly paying the same kind of price to balance against your movements.

I've learned the hard way to check my hula hoop whenever I'm struggling desperately to accomplish some task. The odds are pretty good that I've gotten it hooked over somebody else's stuff, frustrating both of us. Of course, once I notice I've gotten it hooked, I have choices. I can choose to leave things the way they are and just work harder, personally paying the cost in time and energy. I can decide to accept this issue explicitly and move it from their hula hoop into mine, where I can deal with it without having to fight their efforts. I can decide to negotiate, either with them or with the people around us. If we talk about it, we may be able to find ways to work together more smoothly. Maybe I need to ask for more authority, or time, or maybe even a change in the very definition of success. And of course, I may decide to drop this responsibility from my (internal or external) to-do list.

In the real world, we are almost never working with just one other, isolated individual. Each of us is close to many different people—at work, at home, in the community. And each of those individuals has his very own hula hoop, full of his own tasks and responsibilities and cares and joys. No wonder life gets complicated!

The Data Question—What Did You See or Hear?

One of the hardest lessons to learn in life is the difference between perception and reality. We live *in* the world, but by the time our perceptions of a complicated situation get filtered through our senses, personalities, emotions, histories, and preconceived notions, it's a wonder we have any idea of what *really* happened. And it's even worse when we're trying to interact with other people, who of course have their own ideas about what's occurring and what should happen as a result. One of my favorite, most beloved, and certainly most used tools is Jerry's version of The Data Question: "What did you see or hear that makes you . . . ?" I use it every time someone comes up to me all excited about a wrong they want to right. Sometimes, I even remember to use it on myself, when my emotions threaten to run away with a situation.

The Data Question helps me understand what's going on when I get secondhand news, which means I'm less likely to go haring off on an unjustified tangent. And it's even more effective in a group. Groups can accomplish things that would be difficult, if not downright impossible, for an individual. For good . . . or for ill.

Unfortunately, it's not only difficult to remember the difference between our perceptions and reality, it's very human to accept someone else's perceptions (as relayed to us) as our reality. After all, our informant probably *is* very honest and sincere and is telling the truth as he sees it. But now we're at least two layers away from physical reality, with two layers of limited senses, two personalities, and two sets of emotions, histories, and preconceived notions. As in the children's parlor game I learned to play called Gossip, the further away you get from the initial source, the more distortions enter into the message. When a group of people learn to routinely use The Data Question, they are much less likely to ratchet each other up into actions that they will later regret.

You, Me, Nate—Let's All Triangulate . . .

My college professor defined politics as "the art of allocating scarce resources." Heaven knows, the problem of scarce resources is common in most workplaces, and so is politics. And along with politics comes gossip and other unofficial channels of communication; the pushing and shoving and competing for money; and the time and attention that accompany them.

One of the most common interactions in the workplace is when Alice tells Betty something Charlie said. Sometimes, Alice is being malicious, but often enough, Alice is truly trying to be helpful to either Betty or Charlie, and maybe to both. Unfortunately, that doesn't matter. Anytime you see a triangulated interaction forming, you can brace yourself for trouble. Remember the game Gossip again: A message is distorted when it is passed from one person to another; the more people in the chain, the more distorted the message becomes.

There are ways to deal with triangulation, at least in your immediate vicinity. (Unfortunately, you have fewer options when it occurs behind your back.) One of the quickest, most direct responses when you are in Betty's position (the end recipient) is to take Alice gently by the arm (at least figuratively) and offer to accompany her to Charlie so that you can get the message directly from him. If Alice and Charlie are truly trying to be helpful, or at least not malicious, this has a high chance of untangling the situation. If either or both are being consciously malicious, you will at least have a chance to observe the situation with your own senses, unfiltered through another person.

Sometimes, this direct method is not possible. Maybe one of the parties is not physically available, or maybe one or both of them simply refuses to cooperate with your efforts. (They may be embarrassed, or afraid, or simply shy and uncomfortable with possible confrontation.) You still have options, of course. You can discuss Charlie's comments, briefly, with Alice—just enough to suggest that Charlie needs to go directly to you with his concerns. This works occasionally, but it usually isn't optimal, at least in my experience. Better would be to go directly to Charlie and say "I understand that you have some concerns about . . . Can we discuss it?"

Sometimes, even that doesn't work, and Charlie will deny any problems or concerns and refuse to discuss it. Regardless, you should *always* apply The Data Question to get as clear an idea of the situation as possible. And you should remember that you've been triangulated and that this data is at least questionable, if not downright deceptive. Make sure you take that into account when you evaluate the situation and choose a course of action.

As a last resort, when nothing else was working, I've simply refused to listen to Alice's report. Jerry pointed out to me once, when I was very upset about what one Charlie was saying about me behind my back, that Charlie had no real power over me unless I gave it to him. His malicious comments could only hurt me if I listened to them. I tried Jerry's suggestion, out of sheer desperation, I think, and indeed I found myself a lot more relaxed and comfortable at work.

Bet You Can't Change Just One Thing!

However, I was a bit startled when I saw the way the people around me reacted. It seems that sometimes the game of Gossip and the "taking sides against" somebody can become an end in itself: a guilty pleasure that can absorb energy and time that I'd rather be spending on more productive activities.

Some of my coworkers were extremely upset when I told them I had decided to handle Charlie by simply not listening to whatever comments were reported to me. I was happier, but they were very unhappy, at least until they got used to withholding Charlie's negative energy and handling their own stress in other ways. Of course, some of their new ways of behaving reflected back to me, and I had to make adjustments. Balance is a process, never a destination.

The Ultimate Tool

The ultimate tool in your management arsenal is, of course, yourself. It's the one thing you always have available. You can study yourself. After all, you've had a lifetime of practice being yourself. You can study other people—those you admire and hope to emulate, as well as those who act as bad examples in the world around you. You can experiment, try new things, or elaborate and refine some old methods that have been successful in the past. Nobody can take your power over yourself away from you. Even when I'm not wearing my Courage Bracelet, I can feel its ghostly weight upon my wrist, whenever I need the memory.[26]

6

Congruent Feedback

Esther Derby

"Feedback can be defined as information about past behavior, delivered in the present, which may influence future behavior."[27]

Strong and productive working relationships depend on congruent feedback. Without feedback, we don't know where we stand, and we don't know what to adjust. Feedback is one of the primary ways to improve working relationships.

My experience of feedback as an employee didn't match that description. Most of the feedback I received came in the form of evaluation. But evaluation doesn't improve relationships, even when positive ("You are a tenacious problem-solver!"). Nor does evaluation reveal what to adjust.

I met Jerry when working for a large financial services company in the early 1990s. He'd been hired to consult with the Information Services Department. Many of the things I learned from Jerry during that time have made a difference in my life. I have a particularly strong memory of Jerry telling me, "If you can tell a coworker he has BO and he feels you've given him a gift, you can offer feedback about any situation."

I studied Jerry's little book on feedback, and put the Satir concepts he taught me into practice. I've had practice offering feedback about all manner of tricky issues in the workplace. Though the feedback may not always seem like a gift at the moment, it almost always improves a working relationship.

Congruent feedback is not evaluation, criticism, labeling, praise, or blame. It is a genuine effort to improve working relationships and the work itself. Congruent feedback balances the needs and concerns of the person offering feedback (the Self), the person receiving feedback (the Other), and the Context:[28]

Self: The person offering feedback, who wants to improve some aspect of the working relationship.

Other: A colleague deserving of respect and consideration in framing and offering feedback.

Context: The work and the working relationship.

Most of the time, people assume that feedback is negative—that it aims at correcting a shortcoming. But I don't think of feedback as negative (telling someone what's wrong) or positive (telling someone what's good). When feedback is offered in the spirit of improving the working relationship, it's all positive. When we offer feedback, we hope for a change: to increase, decrease, or replace a behavior.

I found having a structure helps me form feedback in a way another person is likely to hear. I use and teach the structure below to help people talk about difficult issues in a way that builds relationships. Using this structure helps keep feedback grounded in facts, respectful, and relevant by bringing conscious attention to Self (the impact of the other person's behavior on me), Other (observable facts, not evaluation about the other person), and Context (our working relationship).

Create an opening that signals that you want to have an important conversation and that establishes a psychological contract to do so. The opening doesn't have to be elaborate—in fact, it's better if it's not. A long windup either confuses the other person or induces dread. Something like, "I'd like to talk to you about the way we're working on this project. Is now a good time?"

It does no good to offer feedback when someone is on his way out the door to catch the bus. And remember, no grant to receive feedback is forever or applies to every topic.

Describe the behavior or events in a way the feedback receiver will recognize. Provide specific, recent examples. Use neutral language. Words that imply evaluation (good, bad) or judgment (lazy, sloppy, irresponsible) can raise defenses rather than spark recognition.

If the feedback receiver doesn't recognize the description, he's not likely to tune in for the rest of the conversation.

State the impact so the feedback receiver understands why he might consider changing his behavior. If you can't articulate the impact, you probably shouldn't be giving the feedback. If there's no impact, a request to change behavior seems arbitrary and petty.

If the impact comes down to personal preference or personal beliefs about how people should act, reconsider why you are giving the feedback. When the behavior doesn't affect the work or the working relationship, think twice, and then think again before you give the feedback.

Make a request. Feedback doesn't mean telling someone what to do or getting someone to change. Feedback is information that a recipient can choose to act on—or not. And it may come with a request. The request may be for joint problem-solving, negotiation, or it may involve asking for a specific action.

I explained the framework in a workshop, one participant was skeptical. "That's too stiff and formal. It wouldn't feel natural to me. I just come out and say what I mean."

I asked the participant to give me an example.

"Last week, my cube-mate had his music on, really loud," he replied, "so I went over to him and said 'Hey, I need to talk to you. When your music is so loud I can hear it through your headset, it drives me crazy and I can't concentrate. Would you turn it down?'"

It was a perfect example. Even though he wasn't conscious of it, he'd covered all the parts of the framework using his own words, and with an informality that fit his relationship with his coworker.

The same framework applies for offering feedback when we want to reinforce a behavior.

A statement such as "That was a good speech" doesn't give information about what specifically was good about the speech (so that goodness can be repeated) or the impact the speech had. A more helpful reinforcing message might be formed as follows:

Opening: "I want to tell you about something that made your speech particularly enjoyable for me."

A description that the person can recognize: "The example you used, to illustrate your point about collaborative requirements, painted a picture for me."

Impact: "It helped me see how I can apply some of the techniques you described with my business partners."

Now the person hearing the feedback has a clear idea of what he did that was helpful to at least one person listening to his speech.

Planning Is Everything

Think through feedback before plunging in, especially if you feel uncomfortable. Make sure you have clear, specific, recent examples from your own experience. Using secondhand examples sets up a tattletale dynamic and erodes trust.

Be sure you can articulate the impact in a way that will make sense to the other person. Be prepared to speak from your own perspective and observation, describing how the behavior affects you or the team. Appealing to vaguely defined standards of behavior—saying, for example, it's not professional or it's not appropriate—won't help. Professional and appropriate are both in the minds of the beholder.

Thinking about what you want to have happen as a result of giving feedback will help you decide what request to make.

Once you've worked through all the parts of the framework, practice. Role-play the feedback or at least say the words out loud so you aren't fumbling when you start the conversation.

The Plan Is Nothing

After you've planned and practiced, be ready to give up your plan. I've seen too many feedback conversations go off the rails because the person offering feedback was determined to finish his speech regardless of how the other person responded.

Consider Jan: She wanted to give Sally feedback, so she planned and practiced her approach. Then she visited Sally.

"Sally," Jan started, "I want to talk to you about the meeting we had with marketing yesterday."

"Oh?" Sally answered. "What's up?"

"Yesterday in our meeting, you jumped in with the technical details three times," Jan continued.

"I wasn't aware that I was doing that!" Sally exclaimed. She seemed surprised at herself, and quickly continued, "I guess it's just habit. Gosh, I'm sorry. I can see where that would be a problem now that you're in the pre-sales technical support role. Thanks for letting me know. I'll try to catch myself next time," Sally said.

"It's going make it harder for marketing to look to me for answers if you jump in," Jan said, plowing ahead. "I'm new to this role, and I need to establish trust with them. When you give all the answers, it's hard for me to build that relationship."

"I totally get it," Sally said. "I'm embarrassed that I was doing that, because I don't want to undercut you."

"I'd like you to stop jumping in with the technical details," Jan finished, feeling rather proud at getting her message out.

"I get it!" Sally snapped. "You don't have to rub my nose in it."

In sales, this is called selling past the close. Salespeople who keep selling once the customer has agreed to buy end up losing the sale. The same will happen when you offer feedback and don't acknowledge the other person's response: Rather than improve the working relationship, you may damage it.

Back-Leading

Sadly, too many people who are in a position to give feedback don't know how. Consider Joe. He was a project manager working on contract. He'd received some upsetting feedback from his client. He looked dejected as he described the feedback he'd received. "They tell me that people from the project team are complaining. They told me I'm a demotivating person," Joe lamented.

Understandably enough, Joe didn't know what to do to improve his relationship with the team or to improve his client's perception of him. How could he? There was no information in the feedback Joe's client gave him.

When you receive feedback that's cryptic or not actionable, back lead. Ask questions to draw out useful information.

Joe might create an opening by saying, "I want to understand this concern. I'd like to ask you some questions so I can decide what to change."

Then, probe for specific, concrete descriptions of behavior: Can you give me an example of things I do that lead to your assessment? Can you tell about a time when my actions had the effect you describe?

In Joe's case, the impact was clear: Some people felt demotivated. That's not always the case. A woman in a workshop reported that her boss told her she was "too nice." She probed for impact by asking, "Can you give me an example of how my style impacts my effectiveness?"

The feedback giver may need a bit of time to pull up examples; a responsible feedback giver will take the time to do so.

If feedback is so important to working relationships, why do people put it off or avoid giving feedback completely?

The (stated) reasons are legion:

- It's not my place.
- I don't want him to feel bad.
- I don't want to embarrass her.
- I'm afraid he'll get angry.
- I'm afraid she'll cry.
- He should know.
- He must know.

None of these is the *real* reason, though. The real reasons are different.

The first one is "I'll be uncomfortable." That's a real possibility. It can be awkward to give feedback. But is the short-lived discomfort worse than the long-term effects? I know of a team that had put off for a year the discomfort of offering feedback to a senior team member, I'll call him Sam, who picked his nose.

During that year, other team members avoided working closely with Sam. And they paid a price. Each team member inhibited his own development by cutting off opportunities to learn from Sam. Because interactions were limited, the team didn't learn about technical problems as soon as it could have, because the team members weren't talking to Sam. They started to resent Sam for "not getting it" when they hinted and made vague statements about hygiene. Sam felt that he was excluded by the team; his engagement in the project dropped.

You be the judge: Which is worse? One uncomfortable conversation or a year of lower productivity, resentment, and hurt feelings?

The second reason cuts closer to the bone: "I'm afraid he/she won't love me if I give feedback." It may seem contradictory, but congruent feedback strengthens working relationships. Congruent feedback indicates that you are invested in the relationship and want it to be better.

7

Solving the Groupthink Problem

Willem van den Ende

Happy birthday, Jerry!

I thought quite a bit about what to write. I asked myself, "What would I like to read, if I were a consultant's consultant and writer, on my seventy-fifth birthday?"

I believe I would like to see that my work has had an impact on the world, and that the things I learned from my elders are being passed on to new generations. An acceptance test for this piece, Jerry, would be that you feel The Law of Raspberry Jam doesn't apply to at least some of your work.

I'll try to combine two things in one piece: to show how I work on a problem that is difficult for me—groupthink—using tools that I learned through Jerry and his lineage, and also to describe the tools.

I've met Jerry only once, so most of the things I learned from him came through his books, his students, and my peers. I'd like to take this opportunity to thank Jerry, and my teachers and peers who have shared their experiences with me.

Enjoy, Jerry, and many happy returns!

Lineage

To paraphrase Jerry's advice, "If all you have is a hammer, the whole world looks like a nail," I offer "If all you have is one teacher, the whole world looks like his models."

Nynke Fokma, a student of Jerry's, introduced me to the concept of a "teaching lineage." In martial arts and shamanism, it is common to refer to your teachers, almost as a way of validating your credibility. If you meet person Y, who has been taught by X, you can go to X and ask about what and how Y learned, as a background check. A lineage is not a line; it's more like a tree of teachers. If you add in the peers, it becomes a densely connected graph.

You can find out about the health of a lineage through the stories its members tell about each other. Nynke, Becky Winant, and Lynne Azpeitia (among others) told me many stories about Jerry and about Virginia Satir, who was a teacher of both Jerry and Lynne. Jerry's books contain many stories about his peers, students, and teachers.

Through them and things I do, I have had the pleasure of meeting many others who are interested in the same things. Some say I am lucky to have so many people around me to share my interests with. Maybe I am. Maybe it is "just" a matter of opening up, sharing your own stories, and thereby attracting the stories of others.

As a student, you gain through your lineage multiple perspectives on the same things: many different stories, tools, models, and experiences with applying these, in various contexts. That helps you to learn in your own way. Learning styles differ, and the right time and way to learn something is different for everyone.

All the stories add up to (at least) one thing: People are human. They make mistakes. There are many ways to laugh about your mistakes, learn from them, and become more fully human.

Below, I describe some tools I learned from my lineage, and then two stories of how I used them. It is not always obvious to me when I learn tools. Good teachers and consultants teach you something in a way that might lead you to believe you've invented it yourself.

Triads

One of the most helpful tools that came through my lineage is the Satir practice of working in triads. Triads help me learn about "people stuff" in difficult times, even when I would rather crawl under a rock than deal with issues.

You may have used triads, because using them comes naturally. If you have two good friends you talk to about recent events, things that puzzle you, problems you are having, then you already have a triad.

I've had a very explicit triad with my friends Nynke Fokma and Marc Evers for a while (and still have, but it has grown more casual). This triad helped me make sense of some groups, as well as of things that were going on in my places of work.

I fondly remember a period when Marc and I drove to work, day by day. Marc would hear me rant about things that were "not going well" (according to me), and then would ask with dogged persistence: "What are three possible interpretations?"

That would be followed by a silence, then one interpretation, then a *long* silence, with me thinking, "I can't come up with another one." Then finally a second and third interpretation.

Developing a triad of interpretations like that helped me to respond more calmly to situations. I tend to think with my emotions sometimes (even though, as I've learned, my mental model is extremely rational).

The reason I believe triads work is that people problems are messy problems. You need to figure out a way that works for *you*. There is no one-size-fits-all solution to problems. Triads give you the opportunity to triangulate—to arrive at a solution for this situation by comparing multiple situations from the past.

Triangulation is opposite to applying "the one best way" (or "best practice") to a situation. And that is the way it should be. You mix the tools, models, and stories you get from your lineage, make them your own, and apply them as best you can to your own problems (first) and (then) to those of your clients and friends.

Virginia Satir's Five Freedoms

I have found the Five Freedoms described by Virginia Satir[29] a very valuable tool:

- the freedom to see and hear what is here, instead of what should be, was, or will be

- the freedom to say what you feel and think instead of what you should

- the freedom to feel what you feel, instead of what you ought

- the freedom to ask for what you want, instead of always waiting for permission

- the freedom to take risks on your own behalf, instead of choosing to be only "secure" and not rocking the boat

Satir's Congruence Model

Finally, I often apply another framework, Satir's Congruence Model.[30]

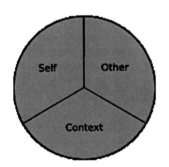

This diagram tells me the balance among Self, Other, and Context as the basis for congruent action. Each part is equally important. I use this model for myself, so Self is me, Other is you, and Context is our family or workplace. I also use it for organizations, so Self is, for instance, a business, Other is its customer, and Context is the market.

When we pay attention to Self, Other, and Context in equal measures, we can act balanced, or congruent. When one or more of these gets little or no attention, we are likely to get trapped in incongruent coping stances.

Let's see how these tools I learned from Jerry and his lineage could be used to help solve a difficult problem.

Groupthink

Have you ever been involved in a group that seems to be going nowhere, but at times makes bold decisions, seems to go somewhere, and then falls flat again? I have.

59

It's frustrating, isn't it? You may have been experiencing groupthink. Groupthink is one of the thornier problems for me. I often fail to detect it, and even when I have, it is not easy to resolve. Groupthink is very easy to fall into, even with an experienced group of people—or maybe especially with experienced and talented people.

Two Stories

Below, I illustrate ways to apply these principles in two stories: One is about dissecting groupthink with a thumbs-up poll; the other is about applying change artistry principles at work.

Stopping the Nonevent

Bob was involved with a group in organizing a first-of-its-kind conference. It was to be a big conference in Bob's home town, for people from across Europe and the rest of the world, on Bob's favorite topic. Bob thought he had a lot of energy for this, and he was eager to work with his colleagues Caroline and Irene. People were already talking about the conference, and if he and his peers didn't put it on, who else would?

After a few months of preparation, Caroline sensed that groupthink was in effect. Bob agreed. The group had not been making much progress, despite some heroic individual actions.

When Bob and Irene discussed the project over drinks, Irene asked what Caroline meant by groupthink. After groping for an explanation, Bob looked it up in Wikipedia, getting this definition:

> "Groupthink is a type of thought exhibited by group members who try to minimize conflict and reach consensus without critically testing, analyzing, and evaluating ideas. During groupthink, members of the group avoid promoting viewpoints outside the comfort zone of consensus thinking. A variety of motives for this may exist such as a desire to avoid being seen as foolish, or a desire to avoid embarrassing or angering other members of the group. Groupthink may cause groups to make hasty, irra-

tional decisions, where individual doubts are set aside, for fear of upsetting the group's balance. The term is usually used pejoratively, with hindsight."[31]

The group had been mulling around for a while, sending e-mails back and forth on what the conference should be about. Bob and some others had started to prepare a vision statement and a budget for the conference. That was completed quickly, but then not much feedback came out of the group. After the budget was more or less prepared, some new members came on board (Bob had tried to grow the group gradually), and they started to ask questions about the conference vision in general, whereas Bob had hoped that the vision would by then be more or less stable and inclusive enough. He felt brainstorming was all well and good, but action was also needed.

On one hand, he did not want to upset the group's balance. But Bob realized that would make him co-responsible for group-think. Maybe it was time to upset the balance, or at least to open the door for doing that. Bob felt that if there were a lack of consensus in the group, it was better to make that lack explicit. Because it seemed that everybody was being very careful to preserve the group's balance, Bob found he could only get a some-what accurate feel for where the group was by talking to all members, one-on-one. Since only Caroline lived nearby, Bob had to do everything over IM, e-mail, and phone, and that was both time-consuming and difficult.

In an attempt to surface the groupthink and get an open discussion going, Bob wrote an e-mail to the group, saying: "I believe we should apply Virginia Satir's Five Freedoms." He listed them, and then continued: "We should accept our differences and use the information that resides inside our frustration (which we will have, sometimes). I prefer to have conflict occasionally over having people simmer on their frustration and eventually leave without warning."

Bob knew that placating was his own favorite incongruent coping stance,[32] sometimes alternating with blaming or out of fear of blaming. And he knew that if his frustration level got high enough, he would suddenly leave a group. He suspected that other group members might have the same preference, and he was getting frustrated. He was having a hard time, as the Dutch saying goes, "of making chocolate out of it."

Bob had frequent IM chats with his triad partners, John and Mary, who were also involved in the conference planning. That helped him get his frustration out, because with John and Mary, he could share his anger and frustration without too many consequences. He had known them both for a couple of years, and they had an eerily good grasp of his thinking and could ask him difficult questions that few other people could (or dared). These chats also helped him pay attention to the context. In a placating mode, context often goes out the window.

In light of the context, Bob thought, "You've taken an option on a conference venue, so if the group doesn't have the energy to pull off the conference, you need to cancel the options." He saw that rocking the boat was necessary. John and Mary helped him balance, so he could rock the boat in a congruent way.

But opening the door to conflict didn't generate the noisy conflict Bob had expected. He got a few responses, not many. At least mentioning the Five Freedoms had given him the confidence to rock the boat.

It still wasn't clear, to him or to the group, whether there was enough energy in the group to pull this conference off. Since he and Caroline were personally responsible for the conference venue, they decided to cancel the option. They realized that if it wasn't clear that there was enough energy, there probably was not.

Canceling the option wasn't the end of everything. The group could still decide to put the conference on at a later time. This took the pressure off and gave them some breathing room.

Bob met a large part of the group at another conference. They got together, and Bob surveyed their energy with a thumbs-up poll. Bob had used the thumbs-up poll in previous situations, to help him detect false consensus, a form of groupthink where people agree for the sake of not rocking the boat. Responses to a question were given and interpreted this way:

Thumbs up: You support the decision and will do everything you can to make it happen.

Thumbs horizontal: You don't care much either way. You will support whatever decision the group makes, but will not put much effort into realizing it.

Thumbs down: You are opposed to the decision.

If people hold their thumb horizontally, they will not block an effort, but they won't go the extra mile to make it happen. If you only ask people to say yea or nay, you may get quite a few invisible horizontal thumbs in the yea camp—those who do not want to upset the group's balance or rock the boat will sometimes say yea to support the people who want to do something. And then, later, the doers will realize slowly and painfully that the yea support has not been followed by action.

When he questioned the group about organizing the conference or not, Bob discovered that most members voted thumbs-horizontal. It turned out that some people just wanted to do something with the group, and the thing itself did not matter much to them.

From the process of trying to get a big conference started, Bob and some other group members discovered that their passion was for small open-space conferences: less overhead, more focus on the topic, and more choice of conference venue. The fact that they were having the discussion at an open-space conference probably influenced this.

Most group members indicated they would support Bob if he had the energy to go forward, but nobody was ecstatic enough about the project to put lots of energy in for its own sake. Bob was honored by people's support, but in the end, he and the group felt that it was better to spend their time on things they had more passion for.

Keeping open the possibility of disbanding the group is, to my mind, the ultimate way to prevent groupthink. People are often afraid to let go of their group, because it is the only thing they have—or so they believe. In my experience, if you have passion for something and want to take responsibility for making it happen, you can always find an existing group, or find people around you who are willing to form a new group to get it off the ground.

Sticking to the group for the group's sake is not likely to build momentum. Quite the contrary. Everyone in the group will be miserable, or indifferent, at best. The group will function as less than the sum of its parts, or even worse, as less than one individual.

If you want a group to continue for its purpose, not just for the sake of the group, consider bringing your change artistry skills to work. Some of the tools mentioned above can now be part of your arsenal. Read on for more of them, and for how to be aware of when you need to use them.

Bring Your Change Artistry Skills to Work

Later, when Bob was working with another group (a not-for-profit foundation around a professional theme), he found he was witnessing discussions on the group's Website going nowhere. Issues involving the stability of the site were not being dealt with. From his previous experience, he had become more comfortable with rocking the boat, so the barrier to doing it again (if necessary) was lower. In this group, some people wanted to discuss strategy first, others (Bob included) wanted to "just do something." Yet others were quiet altogether; maybe they didn't care or didn't have a handle on the situation.

Redesigning a Website that represents a group redefines the group's identity. Pinpoint and resolve conflicts, even unspoken ones, so that you can move on. If you are afraid of upsetting the group's balance, you'll set your individual doubts aside and fall back to groupthink to maintain the status quo.

Bob wanted to preserve the community's memory, and having a Website that went down all the time wouldn't help much. He knew that if they wanted to resolve the strategic issues first, they might never do something about the Website itself. He had rarely experienced effective discussions on strategy, so delaying the Website fix for such a discussion—to be held months later—was risky. But he was stuck on what to do next, so he procrastinated for a couple of weeks.

While he was reading up on cultural patterns of organizations, he stumbled across one of Jerry Weinberg's diagrams of effects:[33]

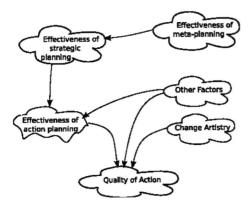

Now he understood why discussions seemed to go past each other. One person wanted to do action planning, another wanted to talk strategy, yet another wanted to talk about the effectiveness of their strategy discussion.

Bob just wanted to do something about the Website. So, he needed some effective action planning and some change artistry to make sure the group would not procrastinate on basics because of undiscussed strategy.

Bob had started to bring some of his change artistry skills to work. His big-conference-planning experience and other community work had convinced him that he couldn't simply be one among peers. To be effective, he needed to apply change artistry everywhere.

The diagram told him that the Quality of Action for the Website would be higher with an effective strategic discussion, which in turn would be effective if there were effective meta-planning. On the other hand, the Other Factors in this case were not to be underestimated. There was a large, diverse, and growing community that was largely invisible to the organizing group. The one thing Bob did know was that the community would complain if the Website went down—so it was time to do something about it.

With the diagram in mind, Bob managed to persuade the others that the strategic discussion was important, but that it did not have to stop work on the Website. The group's reputation would be on the line if the Website went down more often. Therefore, he proposed not to do any new development on the site that would depend on the strategic planning, but at least to invest in transferring the site to a bigger server. This would keep the site live, and the group would then have a stable base to work from, in case participants did decide to make major changes to it.

Bob got the budget for a new server approved and got the improved Website running. How and if the strategic discussion will pan out, the future will tell. Change artistry never ends!

With hindsight, Bob had a flashback and a Doh! moment when he saw the diagram. Other Factors had exerted a lot of influence when he had tried to organize the conference. Everyone had worked part-time on the conference. Most organizers had full-time jobs, they were geographically dispersed, and virtually no-one spoke English as their mother tongue. Worst of all, within the group, there was little experience with organizing conferences for more than one hundred fifty people, so everyone was daunted by the amount of money the sponsoring organization could lose if the conference did not attract sufficient sponsors and attendees. They were also fearful because they suspected there were many things they did not yet know but might learn later, at their own peril.

Conclusion

Change artistry is an endless way of learning. In many ways, peers and teachers are interchangeable. I learn a lot from my students, and as you can see in this essay, I also work together with some of my teachers.

My peers/teachers and some techniques and models helped me get a better grip on groupthink. I still expect to experience groupthink situations occasionally, but I expect I will identify them sooner and respond with more calm and resolve.[34]

8

To Measure Process Improvement, Look at How People Behave

Judah Mogilensky

Once, I was a student of engineering with a poster of Mr. Spock from *Star Trek* on my dorm room wall, a symbol of my belief in pure logic and my discomfort with and distrust of human emotions. It has been a long journey since then, to the point where, when asked to contribute to this volume, my first thought was to write about how people behave. Jerry Weinberg has been a central figure in this journey, along with his wife, Dani, and Jean McLendon. From a chance discussion at an SEI conference, to Consultants Camp, to PSL, to MBTI training, to Congruent Change Shop, to Satir Systems Training, to my return to Congruent Change Shop as an apprentice, to the first AYE—Jerry has been a guiding force, a wise counselor, and a splendid role model. Every time I write an article, give a presentation, or conduct a workshop (especially workshops on MBTI or on Organizational Maps and Sculpts), his influence is there. I am grateful for this opportunity to express my profound appreciation for that influence.

Introduction

An engineering development project, whether in software, systems, or other disciplines, essentially consists of an agreement between the sponsors (also known as gold-owners) and the developers. The agreement typically consists of the following elements: The sponsors agree to provide resources and to describe what they want; in return, the developers agree to deliver a product with a specified set of capabilities, within a specified schedule, for a specified cost, achieving specified levels of quality. Many people in the engineering community have been exposed to the ideas of engineering process maturity (that is, how reliably the developers are able to hold up their end of this agreement) and process improvement (that is, making groups of developers better able to consistently hold up their end of this agreement).

Through the original Capability Maturity Model (CMM) for Software, the current Capability Maturity Model Integration (CMMI) models, and the process appraisal methods associated with them, the Software Engineering Institute (SEI) has introduced and popularized these ideas of engineering process maturity and process improvement. The appraisal methods emphasize evidence, such as documents produced by projects and interviews with people involved in projects and support activities.

In this essay, I describe behavior patterns that I have observed over the years in organizations at different maturity levels. These behavior patterns tend to reinforce and support (or, sometimes, contradict and call into question) the official appraisal data from documentation and interviews. I also describe an unfortunate behavior pattern that—while seeming to comply with the intent of the process models—actually undermines and defeats their purpose. In this way, I hope to provide the reader with signposts to look for in trying to determine whether or not a given process improvement effort is on a likely path toward success.

Before getting into the behavior patterns themselves, I'll give a brief sketch of the process maturity ideas embodied in the models, for those readers not already familiar with them.

Process Improvement and Maturity Levels

The basic idea of process maturity levels was proposed by Watts Humphrey, who built on similar ideas suggested by Phil Crosby. All of the SEI maturity models have the same basic structure of five maturity levels:

Maturity Level 1, the Initial Level, is essentially the default level, before an organization adopts serious process discipline. Success in engineering projects at this level generally results more from the heroic efforts of the people involved, rather than any systematic expectations of the organization about how a project will be planned and executed.

Maturity Level 2, the Managed Level, is the level where procedures and standards are first documented and seriously followed, particularly with regard to project management activities. Efforts to define and enact processes affect such areas as defining and managing changes to project requirements, generating realistic effort and cost estimates, tracking actual project status against plans and taking corrective action when needed, and establishing well-defined baselines of product versions and configurations.

Maturity Level 3, the Defined Level, extends the process discipline to the engineering activities themselves. Efforts to define and enact processes now affect such areas as: eliciting customer and end-user needs beyond the initial requirements statements; identifying major alternative system architectures and systematically choosing the alternative that best meets stated criteria; planning and managing the integration of product components; verifying that the resulting product meets applicable stated requirements; and validating that the resulting product actually achieves the customer's objectives when placed in a realistic operational environment. The process management efforts themselves are now systematically managed as a project, across the whole organization, with each engineering project making use of appropriately tailored versions of guidebooks and templates. The organization ensures, through a system of required training for different roles, that people have the skills and knowledge needed to follow the organization's processes.

Maturity Level 4, the Quantitative Management Level, adds statistical methods to the existing process discipline. Data on process performance are gathered from projects and are used to establish quantitative performance baselines and predictive performance models regarding key aspects of process performance. These baselines and models are then used by individual projects to predict whether quantitative project performance targets will be met, and to take corrective action when predictions suggest those targets are at risk.

Maturity Level 5, the Optimizing Level, adds the expectation that process performance can always be improved. However, improvements should only be introduced after pilot trials have shown that the improvements will have a significant, measurable impact on performance and will preserve the predictability of performance established at Level 4. One form of improvement would be to identify the root causes of recurring or persistent product defects or process problems and eliminate those root causes from the processes.

The maturity models describe the process components of each maturity level. With these components, the organization can undertake a step-by-step approach to achieving more predictable and reliable project performance through process improvement. The maturity models also provide criteria for determining the key strengths and weaknesses of an organization's processes and the maturity level that best describes the organization's current status. Readers desiring more information on these topics are urged to read the original source models and their accompanying literature. (Readers who are familiar with Jerry Weinberg's *Quality Software Management* four-volume series will remember that Jerry defined his own version of these patterns in Volume 1.)

Typical Behavior Patterns at Maturity Levels

The maturity models focus on direct and indirect activities that support engineering projects. Direct activities include project planning, project monitoring and control, requirements development, verification, and validation; indirect activities include measurement and analysis, quality assurance, organizational process definition, and organizational training. Formal appraisal methods put primary emphasis on artifacts and products generated by the projects and support groups (for example, project plan documents, project status reports, requirements analysis reports, quality assurance audit results, organizational training records) and on interviews with project and support group participants.

For example, the Standard CMMI Appraisal Method for Process Improvement, Class A (SCAMPI-A), has clear rules for how the documents are to be gathered and reviewed, how the interviews are to be conducted, and how the evidence is to be examined. Conclusions and results reported by the appraisal team must, according to the method, be based clearly on the evidence provided.

However, my training in the family therapy techniques of Virginia Satir has taught me to treat everything that happens as data, and to look for patterns in the behavior of people. Over the years, this perspective has led me to identify typical behavior patterns encountered in organizations at different maturity levels. Although these patterns are not described in the maturity models and are not treated as evidence by the formal appraisal method, I have found them useful as a way to increase my confidence in the picture presented by the official appraisal evidence or, in some cases, to raise questions about how well the formal evidence reflects the actual current state of the organization's processes.

For example, as a lead appraiser, I frequently deal with the key managers of an organization, the people who sponsor the appraisal. I work with them in negotiating plans for the appraisal, and in dealing with appraisal issues that require management intervention.

When organizations are operating at Maturity Level 1, I often find that it is very difficult to establish a stable schedule for the appraisal; the organization's management almost always asks for at least one postponement, and commonly two or three postponements. I also find that despite my experience conducting appraisals, the managers insist they know better than I do the amounts of time, people, and critical resources needed to conduct their appraisal (and their estimates are always lower than mine). After I give the managers very explicit criteria for selecting suitable team members from within the organization, they almost always respond by proposing at least one or two prospective team members who clearly violate the criteria. In all these ways, the managers demonstrate that the appraisal effort will be treated just like projects within their organizations, that is, with weak process discipline.

Once organizations begin operating at Maturity Levels 2 or 3, the management behavior typically reflects the change. The basic schedule of the appraisal tends to be substantially more stable once it has been set. The managers suggest, at their own initiative, training two-or-three backup team members, in case the planned team members are not available when needed. Perhaps most significantly, the organization prepares its own detailed plan for preparing the appraisal evidence and making the logistical

71

arrangements; this plan is coordinated with my planned activities (such as a readiness review), and progress against the plan is systematically tracked and reported.

Organizations operating at Maturity Levels 4 or 5 also reflect this fact in management's behavior. They have typically not only performed appraisals previously, but they have collected data from those appraisals. They will point out where my estimates are perhaps too optimistic and will suggest adding time or resources. In organizations with lower maturity, the most-senior managers are typically not interviewed, but in high-maturity situations, the very senior managers often need to be interviewed as they have been deeply and directly involved in establishing the organization's statistical measurement approaches.

Management behavior, while a valuable source of maturity-level clues, is not the only source. Another group of people who are central to any appraisal are the participants—that is, the people from the organization who are interviewed. Typically, these people include project managers and key engineers from selected projects, along with representatives of important support groups such as configuration management, quality assurance, procurement, HR/training, and the engineering process group. What these people tell us in the interview sessions is part of the official appraisal data, but how they behave during the appraisal is an important source of unofficial clues.

For example, in Maturity Level 1 organizations, the interview sessions all tend to begin at least five or ten minutes late; some participants arrive at their sessions twenty or more minutes late, and this is treated as nothing unusual. When asked about processes typical of Level 2 organizations, they not only cannot describe what their organization does, but they express surprise that anyone would find it worthwhile to do such things. Typical comments include "Why should requirements be written down if they are just going to change?" and "What would be the point of trying to construct a project plan?" and "Seriously, have you ever seen anyone actually doing this configuration management stuff?" I have come to refer to this phenomenon as "The Wall of Cluelessness." Not only do they not engage in these practices, but they are clueless about why anyone would do so.

By contrast, in Maturity Level 2 or 3 organizations, people tend to be very punctual for their interview sessions; those who do come at all late apologize profusely for doing so. The participants can not only describe their processes, but they do so with notable pride and enthusiasm, and with confidence in the value of these processes. Particularly in Level 3 organizations, the terminology used and the mechanisms described are very consistent; team members sometimes complain that the interviews become "boring" because everyone is describing the same things in the same way. There is still a Wall of Cluelessness, but now it applies to higher-level activities; typical comments include "How could you establish statistical baselines for process performance?" and "What kinds of predictive models do people build?"

Finally, in Maturity Level 4 or 5 organizations, the enthusiasm and confidence extend to the discussions of key measures and how they are analyzed. Participants often bring tables, charts, and graphs with them to the interview sessions, and they are able to explain in detail what they mean. Almost every interview session reveals a new story about a process improvement or new tool that has been or is about to be piloted by the participants. Project teams or support groups describe with pride their roles in piloting innovations, and they describe competing with each other for the privilege. Most significantly, the appraisal team discovers that nearly every process weakness it identified has already been noted by the organization itself, and process improvement activities are already either planned or underway, to address those weaknesses.

A third source of behavioral clues, apart from organizational management and the appraisal interviewees, is the appraisal team members themselves. The rules for process improvement appraisals require that at least one person on the team be from the organization being appraised; common practice is to have roughly half of the team consist of members of that organization. (The others may be from other groups or divisions within the same corporate family, or they may be complete outsiders.) As lead appraiser, I spend a lot of time with the team members, both in team training and during the conduct of the appraisal, so I get to view the internal team members as an informal sample of typical organizational behavior.

Again, the pattern is very similar. In organizations operating at Maturity Level 1, it is not unusual for team members to come late at the start of the day, during team training, and to come back late from breaks. (They typically do maintain a strong interest in when the training session will end for the day, and they seem surprised when I assert that the ending time depends, to some extent, on when we start.) Team members working in small groups will often struggle for a long time over a model interpretation issue, or over what kinds of additional evidence to ask for, rather than asking my opinion and moving on. Although I try to make clear what work the team should be completing each day, the team members typically fall well behind schedule, and I end up having to adjust the work distribution or the activity schedule in order to catch them up. (This last problem can happen even with higher maturity organizations and their teams, depending on how well prepared the organization's evidence is, but it practically always happens with teams from low-maturity organizations.)

When the team members come from Maturity Level 2 or 3 organizations, I typically see solid, on-time behavior, both during training and during the on-site event. When model interpretation issues or other questions arise, the team members bring them to me much more quickly, so confusion and doubt do not eat up large amounts of time. Team members track the progress of their own work, and they volunteer to stay late when they need to catch up (or, if their work is finished, they may volunteer to stay and help other team members finish their work). At least one team member works on collecting data on appraisal efforts and progress, for use in planning future appraisals. In addition, team members are focused on recording improved guidelines for evidence preparation and other lessons learned regarding the conduct of appraisals.

When an organization is operating at Maturity Levels 4 or 5, the team is typically very well-experienced, with no first-time team members. The members are well prepared for their roles, and they are very focused on maintaining the needed pace of work. If team members fall behind schedule, they take steps to catch up, often without prompting from me. They also often look for ways to get ahead of schedule, by getting an early start on some of the later tasks.

Of course, as a practicing lead appraiser, I don't want to give away all my secrets, so this has been just a partial list of behavioral indicators that I look for. I also must emphasize that I am looking for consistent patterns across the management, participant, and team member groups. A single, isolated instance of any behavior may not be particularly significant. I also want to emphasize that the official data, that is, the evidence consisting of documents from projects and statements in interviews, is still the only basis for arriving at the formal results of a SCAMPI-A appraisal. But I do find it very useful to have these behavioral indicators as confidence builders (or as red-flag raisers), and I have encouraged my fellow lead appraisers to develop their own behavioral indicators.

The "Dark Side" of Process Improvement

My observations of behaviors in organizations undertaking model-based process improvement have led me to identify another phenomenon, one that is not widely recognized or acknowledged (at present, anyway) within the SEI process community. One of the key underlying premises of all of the maturity models is that adopting the practices in the model will lead to improved project predictability, higher productivity, and increased product quality. While many organizations have achieved and measured these benefits, there are persistent stories of organizations that have been formally rated at high maturity levels without showing the corresponding performance improvement expected of them. One theory is that this problem results from lead appraisers not being well-enough trained in or familiar with the intended interpretation of the maturity models, especially for Maturity Levels 4 and 5. As a result, new training and new testing have been provided for lead appraisers.

While this theory clearly has some basis, and while the steps being taken are definitely helping to address the problem of high maturity ratings not resulting in expected performance improvement, I do not believe that deficiencies in lead appraiser training and knowledge are the only problems involved. My belief, based on my observations of behavior patterns, is that another part of the problem is a phenomenon that (with apologies to *Star Wars)* may be viewed as the "dark side" of the process improvement "force." I call it Pathological Box-Checking.

Pathological Box-Checking can take root in an organization when the objective of achieving some maturity level rating is seen as the primary organizational goal, and anything that interferes with this goal, or puts it at risk, is seen as an obstacle to be over-come. What separates Pathological Box-Checking from true process improvement is that the latter puts primary emphasis on measurable project performance, measurable business perfor-mance, customer satisfaction, employee satisfaction, and contin-uous improvement. Pathological Box-Checking, on the other hand, views maturity level ratings as the ultimate objectives and seeks to achieve them even if the result has negative impacts on project performance, business performance, customer and employee satis-faction, and continuous improvement. Again, as with the maturity levels, it is characteristic behaviors that indicate this pattern and suggest that organizations following this unfortunate path will hardly ever see any organizational performance benefit from achievements in maturity level ratings.

There are a number of visible symptoms suggesting that a so-called organizational process improvement effort has really "gone over to the dark side" and become Pathological Box-Checking. For example,

- Maturity level targets and associated dates are widely publi-cized and discussed, but there is little or no corresponding publicity and discussion devoted to project or business perfor-mance targets and their associated dates.

- A lead appraiser is brought in because he or she is seen as an "easy grader" or a "flexible rater" (if not a "generous rater"), while actual expertise and experience are seen as secondary (if not irrelevant). Lead appraisers who are known to recognize Pathological Box-Checking are particularly avoided.

- A lot of time and energy is devoted to determining the "minimum acceptable" process implementation that will result in a rating of "Satisfied," regardless of the process actually needed by projects or the organization. In severe cases, organi-zational advocates (even the organization's lawyers) will loudly order the lead appraiser to point out "where in the model it explicitly says that I have to do something."

- Because the focus is on achieving maturity level targets as quickly as possible, there is "no time" for broad participation, review, or piloting new processes. Instead, the processes are developed by a small group or even imported from outside; then they're imposed on groups and projects with little regard for suitability or applicability. Objections to these processes are viewed as "resistance to be overcome." Feedback is discouraged; again, there is "no time" to update or revise processes in response to user experiences.

- Alternative practices are viewed as "too risky" ("What if the lead appraiser doesn't agree with them?") and are effectively, though usually not explicitly, prohibited. (Maturity models provide flexibility to organizations by allowing "alternative practices," that is, practices that differ from those stated in the model, but that better suit an organization's circumstances and contribute equivalently to satisfying the model's goals.) Choices are always made in the direction of the most literal possible implementation of model practices, with little regard for suitability or applicability.

- When a formal appraisal is planned, great effort is devoted to drawing the line around the "organizational scope" in a way that includes only the "good" projects and avoids projects that may put results at risk—even if the scope does not follow natural business or organizational boundaries. Alternatively, the organizational scope line is drawn in a natural way, but certain "bad" projects are hidden from the view of the lead appraiser, perhaps only to be discovered by accident during the on-site period, perhaps never to be discovered.

- Once a formal appraisal, or perhaps even an informal appraisal, has been conducted and a particular process is rated as "Satisfied," changes to that process are effectively, though again usually not explicitly, prohibited. (The thought behind this is, "If we change it, the lead appraiser might not rate it the same anymore.") In this way, the stated model objective of continuous process improvement is essentially abandoned.

While any one of these, or similar symptoms, might not signify much by itself, a pattern of several of them together indicates, in my view, that the organization is no longer engaged in true process improvement, but rather has gone over to the dark side of Pathological Box-Checking. In reality, this is a tragic result for the organization, because it will spend a lot of time and energy and may even be awarded a coveted target maturity level, but the organization will see little or no benefit in its performance. Indeed, I believe that many of the cases where people report that "this organization says that it has a formal rating of Maturity Level X, but it does not behave like it" result from Pathological Box-Checking. Unfortunately, the SCAMPI-A appraisal method is not necessarily designed to distinguish between true process improvement and Pathological Box-Checking.

However, those of us who believe in model-based true process improvement can learn to recognize the difference in the organizations we work with. Each of us can examine the situations we work in and make our own judgment about which side of the process improvement "force" we are on. We can educate our managers and sponsors about the seductive nature of the dark side and of the perils associated with it. And we can make our own choice about where we stand. I hope you will join me in the campaign against Pathological Box-Checking. And I hope that the broader process improvement community will come to recognize that the behavior of people, even more than the paper trail of documents, is the real indicator of an organization's process maturity.

9

The Wisdom and Value of Experiential Learning

Naomi Karten

During a conference session I attended recently, I looked around the room as the speaker read from bullet-item-laden slides to an audience seated in rows, grade-school-like. I saw three people on their BlackBerrys, four repeatedly checking their cell phones, one scanning a magazine, and one surreptitiously doing a Sudoku puzzle. I've no doubt these people were at least half-listening; rarely in a presentation or class is it necessary to hang onto every word. And for some topics, this passive, you-talk-I-listen approach to learning is appropriate.

But for developing critical organizational skills such as communicating effectively, building relationships, handling challenging situations, carrying out projects, and functioning as a leader or team member, nothing surpasses experiential learning. Note: experiential *learning*, not experiential training. In experiential learning, students are fully engaged, and as a result, *they* determine what they learn, not the instructors or presenters. Indeed, it is more appropriate to refer to them as participants rather than students, since they are actively involved, not passive listeners.

Experiential learning revolves around the use of simulations—activities designed to mimic real-life situations. In a successful simulation, students behave much as they would in the actual situation. In doing so, they have an opportunity to learn about themselves and others, and what they learn tends to have staying power.

Not that experiential learning is necessarily a simple matter. Pilots in training take part in flight simulation, an expensive, time-consuming, and technology-intensive approach to learning; simulation ensures that pilots have mastered the complexities of flight before taking us aloft. Happily, most simulations designed to foster learning of interpersonal and organizational skills can be carried out in mere hours, at minimal cost, and without any special technology.

How Simulations Work

Although I've always used experiential exercises in my own seminars, it was through my several years as an instructor in Weinberg and Weinberg's Problem Solving Leadership (PSL) workshop that I gained a deep understanding of how to do it well. Created by Jerry and Dani Weinberg, the five-and-a-half-day PSL workshop is a powerhouse of experiential learning opportunities for participants—and for instructors as well.

In one PSL simulation known as House of Cards, teams created only a few hours earlier are given a successive set of construction projects. Just as often happens at work, most teams are so eager to complete their projects that they fall into familiar traps, such as making assumptions about project requirements, feeling unduly pressured by time constraints, rejecting each other's ideas, taking control, and failing to learn from obvious mistakes.

Instead of offering this simulation, we could have lectured on how to work well as a project team. But generic how-to's don't necessarily translate well into application in the workplace. In House of Cards, people actively participate. In so doing, they often behave in counterproductive ways that mirror their behavior at work. Their firsthand experience sets the stage for discussion and reflection about how they contribute to the outcome and what they can do, as individuals and as a team, to ensure a better outcome in the future.

In another PSL simulation, known as VerseWorks, participants role-play as employees in a company whose mission is to create a product and sell it to the market at a profit. This four-hour-long simulation is chockful of potential for conflict, miscommunication, abrupt priority changes, differences of opinion, confusion about requirements, and lots and lots of chaos. But this potential exists not because of obstacles deliberately put in the way of participants, but rather because the simulation offers a microcosm of the foibles and fumbles of real-world organizations. Indeed, many participants comment afterward that this experience is strikingly like what they experience at work.

In well-designed simulations, people act as they would in analogous real-life situations. As a result, the underlying goal of VerseWorks is not whether the company earns a profit or not, but what people learn about themselves and each other in the course of striving to succeed.

Learning from Leading

If being a participant in a simulation like VerseWorks is a challenge, so too is being an instructor facilitating the simulation. One of many things I learned from Jerry was to follow the energy. You never know what direction an experiential activity is going to take. People are endlessly creative and take the activity in directions of their own choosing. One dramatic example of this occurred when Fiona Charles took PSL: She quit the VerseWorks company and she and a coconspirator formed their own company to compete with VerseWorks, a move I had never before seen. Jerry and I immediately adapted to the move and worked with it.

For the VerseWorks simulation, my co-instructors and I played roles that interacted with the VerseWorks "employees." Initially, as a new PSL instructor, I thought I was supposed to role-play in a way that would make things difficult for the participants, to spur them to find ways of coping. With Jerry's guidance, I quickly learned that my responsibility was just the opposite: to guide their learning, not interfere with it. But even when I tried to be helpful, providing information and answering questions (always within the context of my assigned roles), VerseWorks employees seemed to get tangled in repeated snafus. Indeed, we human beings have a way to making a mess of things. But what better place to gain insight into those messes and how to avoid them than in a simulation?

For several years, we ran the VerseWorks simulation in two adjacent meeting rooms with certain functions assigned to each room, much as the functions of any company are spread over floors, cities, or countries. Then, during one workshop, Jerry proposed that we run VerseWorks in a single, small, meeting room. I was sure that with everyone in physical proximity, easily able to see and hear each other, the communication snags common in the two-room version wouldn't emerge. The VerseWorks company would achieve rapid and certain success and participants would miss out on the opportunity to learn from this simulation.

Jerry urged me not to worry, saying, "Being in one room won't change a thing." I worried anyway. I needn't have. Information still went astray. Small though the room was, key documents somehow got lost. Just as in the two-room version, people misinterpreted critical details or failed to inform those who needed to know. And, just as in the two-room version, they ignored or discounted each other's ideas, and at times treated each other unkindly in the push to succeed.

The beauty of this simulation was that it didn't seem to matter what we did to help. In one running of VerseWorks, an instructor posted a process flow diagram that showed a series of steps that would help the company achieve profitability. One fellow looked at it, shrugged his shoulders, and walked away. No one else even looked at it. In another running of VerseWorks, an instructor handed a similar workflow diagram directly to one of the participants—who proceeded to lose it under a pile of paper.

The moral: People are relentlessly themselves. Whether in real life or in a simulation of real life, their strengths and abilities accompany them everywhere, balanced by their weaknesses, flaws, and limitations.

Debriefs

The active nature of most simulations prevents people from observing their own behavior, especially when they're feeling stressed or challenged. For a simulation to be useful to participants, they must have a chance afterward to debrief—to reflect on their experiences and determine what they learned. The debrief also gives participants the opportunity to reflect as well as to learn about other people's experiences and how those experiences match—or differ from—their own.

Debriefing can take numerous forms and, in PSL, the debrief varies with each simulation. In the House of Cards simulation, the debrief took the form of a final project: Teammates spoke as a group, identified as many lessons learned as they could, and documented those lessons—and Oh, they had only five minutes for this. Yet, even in only five minutes, most teams quickly created long lists of lessons learned. Brief as this type of debrief was, it enabled people to surface learnings that might otherwise have simply floated away on a cloud of fatigue.

By capturing a written list, participants came to appreciate what they learned that they didn't realize they had learned. They learn even more when each team recites its lessons learned—an excellent component of this type of debrief because it shows that no team is alone in facing problems, making mistakes, and struggling to overcome challenges. Reporting out also reinforces the idea that publicly discussing what's gone wrong is a key step in ensuring a better outcome next time.

Five minutes may be fine for debriefing certain types of simulations. In others, an entire day may be more appropriate. That was the case with VerseWorks. After a four-hour-long simulation in which many participants experience stress, frustration, annoyance, and confusion, Jerry rightly felt that people need ample time and many avenues to gain insight into their experience and what they learned from it. But not till the next day.

For VerseWorks, we selected from multiple debriefing options. In one, the entire group sat in a circle and each person in turn said something about his or her experience in the simulation. We went around the circle again and again till everyone surfaced whatever thoughts and feelings they wanted to share. This type of debrief ensured that everyone's experience had a fair hearing. And Jerry, always a keen observer, helped people see patterns of behavior that they were too immersed in the activity to see themselves.

In another activity designed to debrief VerseWorks, participants identified instances of miscommunication during the simulation that seemed to ruffle feathers or lead to problems. We then used one of several communication techniques to debug the flow of information and find when and how it went awry. This debrief not only helped people make sense of some of the communication snafus that transpired during VerseWorks, it also demonstrated a technique that people could apply back at work when miscommunications occurred.

A third debriefing activity, powerful because of its visual nature, was to have people take long strands of lightweight rope, tie one end loosely around their waist, and tie the other end lightly around the rope attached to the waist of each person with whom they interacted during the simulation. Most of the time, we are only aware of our own interactions. But now, through the tangle of intertwined ropes, everyone could grasp the number and complexity of interactions. No wonder there was so much confusion! And no wonder certain people seemed so stressed: Just look at all the people who interacted with them, each with his or her own demands!

My favorite debriefing activity after VerseWorks is called Art Gallery. In this activity, people gather into "affinity groups," each consisting of people who worked together during the VerseWorks simulation. Each affinity group is given colored markers and a sheet of flipchart paper and is asked to draw something that depicts their experience as VerseWorks employees. And they have to draw in silence. No talking.

When the allotted time is up, each affinity group posts its sheet of flipchart paper on the wall, indeed creating an Art Gallery. Then, one at a time, the people in each group take turns describing their group's masterpiece.

What people come up with is breathtaking. Their drawings speak volumes about how *they* experienced things. It's easy to underestimate the intensity of the experience of someone who claims to feel trapped or to be facing terrible pressure; seeing a visual depiction of that trap or that pressure leaves no doubt.

These images capture, as words alone cannot, the frustrations, chaos, confusion—as well as the joy and delight—that people experience. And the art show, overall, emphatically demonstrates the vast differences in people's experiences, depending on the function they had performed for the VerseWorks company, how they were treated as employees, and how much control they had over their work and their very lives.

At first, I didn't care for Art Gallery; I felt myself to be so artistically challenged that I didn't want to foist on someone else what I didn't like doing myself. But Art Gallery was a favorite of Jerry's, so I agreed to it. Over the course of many workshops Jerry and I co-led, I came to see the beauty of Art Gallery as a debriefing technique. So much of what we do in organizations—and in work-shops and presentations—is cerebral, left-brained, analytical, word-oriented, written, spoken, thinking, thinking, thinking. Art Gallery gives people an opportunity and an outlet to look at their experience differently, wordlessly.

Unexpected Experiential Learning

Jerry and I were co-instructors for the PSL that ran in Albuquerque the week of September 10, 2001. On the morning of September 11, we learned that the unimaginable had happened—the twin towers of the World Trade Center in New York City had been attacked and were destroyed, presumably the act of terrorists. The news was terrifying and devastating. PSL participants gathered in shock in our meeting room and talked, cried, shared fears and hopes, caring for each other by just being together. If flights had not been grounded, I have no doubt we all would have immediately gone home. But we couldn't. At length, Jerry and I reached the difficult decision to proceed with the workshop, agreeing to make adjust-ments as needed to accommodate people's needs to be alone or together, to talk or remain silent, to participate or just observe.

My plan for the morning of the 11th was to present Virginia Satir's change model, which explains the turbulent, unsettling experience of chaos that people face when confronted with signifi-cant change. But instead of the organizational situations that participants usually identify as examples of change, we talked about the devastating events of the day. Real life had intervened to give experiential learning an unexpected and unwanted twist.

After a while, Jerry saw that we needed to do something physical as a break from the emotional intensity we all felt. He had us engage in a playful, childlike, physical activity, moving around, taking verbal potshots at each other, laughing, and truly behaving like kids. The sheer physicality was just the release everyone needed.

This child's play was an experiential activity done without Jerry's having announced it as such. And it was its own debrief. Once we stopped, we realized that child's play had given all of us a much-needed break from the intensity that preceded it and that certainly would follow it. Jerry helped us to understand that even in the midst of horror, being able to interact in simple play and to laugh a little is more than just a coping strategy; it is a life preserver.

One–Minute Experiential Learning

Most of the experiential activities in PSL span hours. But experiential learning can take place in minutes. In my Managing Customer Expectations seminar, I explain that people who are listening sometimes look like they're *not* listening, and that look may discourage their customers from providing critical information.

To help participants get this point viscerally, I have the group divide into pairs. In each pair, one person is dubbed the Speaker, and the other, the Listener. I then ask the Speakers to select a topic that's of particular interest to them and to speak about it to their Listener. And I direct the Listeners to display visible signs of being bored, distracted, and uninterested. After one minute, I have them swap roles, so that everyone has the experience of being both a Speaker and a Listener.

When asked to exhibit non-listening, people are wonderfully imaginative, and laughter fills the room. I then ask the group how it was for them when they were the Speaker in the pair. Despite the laughter, people report being frustrated, stressed, and even angry as Speakers. Many claim they just wanted to stop talking: Why continue when the other person doesn't care? Even though this simulation is a contrived activity designed to make a point— and an obvious point, at that—people experience strong emotions, something not likely to happen in a Ten Tips for Better Listening lecture.

To transform the negative experience into a positive one, I close this segment of the seminar with one additional simulation in which each Listener exhibits clear signs of truly listening. But what transpires is no longer a simulation; now, it's a genuine conversation. With the gut-level—and sharply contrasting—experience of both being listened to and being *not* listened to, participants become committed to paying attention to their own listening behavior.

In this listening simulation, I overtly present an activity. In other simulations, people are led into the activity without realizing it. This is an approach I often take in my presentation Changing How You Communicate During Change. Several minutes into the presentation, I ask people to gather their materials and move to another seat. There's a bit of hustle and bustle as people move around. When they've settled in, I ask them, "How was it for you when I asked you to change your seat?"

Some people don't mind changing their seat. Others may be intrigued, glad, annoyed, resentful, or any of numerous other reactions. I recall one agitated fellow who said he had arrived early to find a seat where he could plug in his computer and was unhappy when he had to move. Another participant said he sat close to see the screen better and didn't want to move. A third said he'd been in a wobbly chair and was glad to be able to change seats. A fourth had wanted an aisle seat and now he had it.

As mild and innocuous as this simulated organizational change is, it generates felt reactions. And as people describe their reactions, it becomes obvious to everyone that they have had a multitude of different reactions. Instead of hearing me claim that people react differently to change, they experience that fact first-hand. And they do so without my announcing that I am about to stage a simulation and then a debrief of that simulation.

Later in the presentation, before I discuss how most people eventually adjust to a change, I ask people how they feel about their new seats. Most report being just fine. Some are less pleased. Some like the new seat better. These reports support and reinforce the points I proceed to make about adjusting to change.

I learned from Jerry that you never know where opportunities for learning will come from. That was once the case when I asked people to move to new seats, and then asked them how the "move" was for them. One fellow commented that he had arrived late. When he saw everyone "milling around," he thought with relief that the session hadn't started yet and he wasn't late after all, perfectly illustrating how people who join an organization after a change very likely have a more cerebral, less visceral, experience of that change than the people who lived through it. This man's comment led to a discussion of the role of empathy for those who have been through a major change by those who come along afterward.

Learning, Not Being Taught

Standard course descriptions often use wording such as, "In this course, you will learn," followed by a list of bullet items. By contrast, listings for experiential courses don't tell students what they will learn, because they will learn whatever they most need to learn. This is often very different from what we might predict.

I discovered that fact firsthand in one of my seminars. As an after-lunch energizer, I gave out a paper-and-pencil puzzle and invited students to take a few minutes to work on the puzzle. At the end of the allotted time, a man in the group asked, "Why did you give us this exercise?" Thinking he'd be disappointed to know I had no content-related objective, I answered his question with one of my own: "Why do you *think* I gave it?" To my amazement, he identified a lesson he learned from the puzzle exercise that related to material we had spent the morning on. I then asked the others what they had learned from the exercise. They too offered lessons learned based on the morning's material.

What a surprise this was for me! Students saw this puzzle exercise as emphasizing the key points we had covered during the morning. This was experiential learning of the most unplanned kind. Thereafter, following every after-lunch energizer, I ask participants, "Now why do you suppose I gave you this exercise?" Time after time, they relate the exercise to the material we covered in the morning, indisputable proof of Jerry's contention that people learn whatever they are most ready to learn.

During the years I co-led PSL, we sometimes ran concurrent PSL workshops in adjacent meeting rooms, each with its own two instructors. Invariably, people asked us how we decided who would be in which class. Jerry liked to respond that we carefully grouped people who we thought would learn the most from each other. Because, indeed, in experiential learning, much of what people learn is not from the instructors or even from the activities per se, but from each other.

Of course, the truth is that the assignment of students to the two groups was random: one to this class, one to that class, back and forth, till we went through the entire list. We knew—because this is an essential truth of experiential learning—that it didn't matter which of the two groups anyone ended up in. They'd each learn what they were ready to learn and their classmates, know-ingly or unknowingly, would contribute to their learning. As Jerry rightly emphasizes, in experiential learning, everyone is a teacher and everyone is a student.

The Challenge of Describing Experiential Learning

Experiential learning is difficult to explain to those who haven't experienced it. You can say, "We take part in simulations and discuss what we learn." But that doesn't quite capture it. And indeed, PSL is a case in point: It's almost impossible to describe to people who haven't attended. When I first heard about PSL and was considering enrolling, I asked prior attendees what happened in it. Rather than answer, they would just smile. Those smiles scared me. Whatever PSL was, I decided I didn't want any part of it. But after years of encouragement from Jerry and Dani, I gave in. I came out of the experience wearing the same big smile. Six months later, I accepted their invitation to become an instructor.

As a PSL instructor, I discovered that many people attending had the same suspicion I'd had prior to attending: that people who had attended must have been sworn to secrecy. They, like me, couldn't understand why no one would reveal anything. So, when I became an instructor, I introduced The Taking of the Secret Oath, which I administered at the end of the workshop, saying,

"Repeat after me: 'I swear . . . that when I return home . . . and people ask me what happened at PSL . . . I will tell them . . . absolutely . . . positively . . . whatever I want.'"

But no one really needed to be sworn to secrecy. Even if anyone could fully describe experiential learning in the context of PSL, no one wanted to spoil anyone else's experience, knowing full well that experiential learning gives you your own experience, not someone else's.

As one of our closing activities at the end of PSL, we would invite participants to ask us questions. Often, they had questions about various aspects of the workshop and how previous groups had responded to some of the activities. Sometimes, someone would ask what our lasting memories of their particular group would be. For me, this question was easy to answer because there were always special moments during each workshop that I knew would stay with me. Jerry would respond simply: He had no way of knowing—at the moment—what memories would last.

One answer I should have given was that the experience of partnering with Jerry for each extraordinary week-long workshop would be a lasting memory. In true Jerry-style, I suppose I have to acknowledge that I have no way of knowing now that I'll have this memory forever. But I'm quite sure I will.

10

Reflecting on a Workshop Called Problem Solving Leadership

James Bullock

When you first start training in aikido, it is the tricks that hook you. It looks like magic, which it is: consciously executed technique, refined through practice, applying models of human interaction, to manage those interactions. Magic. Aikido becomes more real and more strange when you try it. Beginners who try it are always startled the first time they feel an aikido technique with their own body, and are amazed the first time their own technique works. The experience just raises more questions. When you see but don't understand, know but can't do, or sense a problem but not a solution, you've encountered something important that you can't use all the time.

PSL is like that.

PSL is an experiential, residential workshop lasting about a week. It uses immersion and simulation to introduce interaction models that are particularly effective for people developing systems. The content is delivered by example and simple handouts. The simulations are supported by reflection and feedback, along with optional one-on-one consulting. Several of the models are unique. All are effective. At the end of the workshop, the students receive *Becoming a Technical Leader,* a handbook for the kind of leadership practiced in the workshop.

That keyword description misses the point. PSL introduces a different system describing what you thought you knew about teams working together on problems that look technical. Memorizing the models is trivial. Anyone successful in systems work could memorize the PSL models in an hour. It is harder to make them available in real time to professionals practicing their craft. Learning to use them when you need them takes forever. A week is barely enough time to get started.

The PSL approach to learning resembles aikido and the other martial "ways" of Japan. PSL, like aikido, is based on exercises: the reflective practice of techniques and prescribed forms. PSL and the martial ways use an environment designed for demonstration, practice, and reflection to teach principles through techniques. Interacting with the forms and with others within the forms, principles emerge. PSL doesn't really make the distinction between theory and practice. Neither does aikido. To know is to do.

From flying planes to dance, high performance is taught through example and practice. Lecture and interrogation aren't enough. Even in education itself, graduate students work with scholars actively doing scholarship versus talking about scholarship with a quiz every Tuesday. Problem-solving with technical teams is a high-performance practice, not a written test at a desk. An expression from medieval Japan—"He smells of leaves"—refers to one who reads, and talks, and thinks, and doesn't do. This is scholarship, not leadership. Expert test-takers "smell of leaves." PSL is about practicing doing.

Before the modern martial ways like aikido, there were combat forms with names ending in *jitsu*, literally meaning "technique." So *aiki-do, ju-do,* and *ken-do* had predecessors: *aiki-jitsu, ju-jitsu,* and *ken-jitsu.* The *jitsu*'s were developed for combat, but the *do*'s emerged for personal development. The PSL content comes mainly from family therapy, and partially from general systems, psychology, and learning theory. In PSL, there are communication modes, personality types, communication tools, and change models. Aikido teaches movement, grounding, energy, and extension. Both aikido and PSL teach principles and techniques initially developed to be more effective when it mattered, sometimes in life or death situations. The insights were developed because they were needed, and the transmission methods emerged because they work. Both PSL and aikido teach a practiced awareness of oneself, the situation, and others. The original *jitsu* "techniques" cultivated practitioners' awareness, for effectiveness in combat. The modern *do* "ways" practice effectiveness to cultivate awareness. The practice shapes the practitioner. PSL is like that.

The similarity in methods—from different times, cultures, and practices—suggests something basic about how people learn. There are, I think, four keys to learning through experience. They are at least common to the design of PSL and the martial ways:

> *Simulation:* Learning through simulation involves a designed experience that extracts and highlights some aspect of reality. Moved out of their homes, businesses, and careers, PSL participants are as removed from the background of their lives as *aikidoka* (pronounced "eye-key-doe-kah," meaning "aikido practitioners") on the mat. They experience the pure encounter, without distraction.

> *Modeling:* PSL, the *jitsu*'s, and the *do*'s use demonstration. A technique can never be completely described, never completely recorded. The essentials of a practice are communicated by one person observing, another showing: "Like this." The catalogs of transmission in the classical *budo* (pronounced "boo-doe," meaning "martial ways") and *bujitsu* (pronounced "boo-jit-sue," meaning "martial techniques") are cryptic. They are more like notes than lectures: reminders of what was learned versus original sources. The PSL faculty show, rather than describe. The description is not the thing.

> *Participation:* There are no students in PSL, only participants. Like in the *do*'s and the *jitsu*'s, people in PSL practice. They do not sit in lectures or watch the art. The student pose is fundamentally remote and judging, evaluating from a safe distance. There is little humility in a disengaged critic, even one called a student. But, when you practice, you are the subject. PSL is mostly participation. The detached pose is shattered. The practitioner is the encounter being studied.

> *Balanced Reflection:* Reflection is part of PSL and

93

aikido. In aikido and the ways, awareness and reflection are developed through meditation, demonstration, and practice. The habit of active reflection eventually extends to execution even under stress. Proper technique contains *zanchin* (pronounced "zan-shin"). One translation is "perfect finish." Another is "remaining mind." *Zanchin* means showing the active reflection that was there before and throughout the technique. It becomes a way of life. Real problem-solving is continuously reflective.

Aikido is an outstanding analogy for PSL because both are about the principles of human interactions. Aikido practices techniques, mainly joint locks and throws, designed to illuminate the principles behind the techniques. Like a *dojo* (pronounced "doe-joe," meaning literally "place of the way"), PSL creates a microcosm where fundamental, subtle realities are on display. Science works this way. Gases contracting are difficult to know as an experience, yet the parlor trick of sucking an egg into a milk bottle shows the abstract idea in terms of action in the world. The barrenness of the dojo floor leaves the pure encounter with its principles exposed. With just you and another *aikidoka* alone on a featureless white mat, there is nowhere to hide. The egg gets sucked into a bottle, and you can perceive directly a process that has always been there, unseen.

Science, aikido, and magic teach by managing awareness of the egg. In learning to develop leadership, you are the egg. One doesn't encounter a different way to interpret the world without interpreting the world that way. The martial ways are about encounters between people on and off the dojo floor. We can learn, if we choose, to approach any encounter as an expression of problem-solving leadership or as *ai-ki-do,* the "way of blending energy," more or less. Our awareness of problem-solving or aikido in any encounter is our choice. It's up to us to choose to see the egg.

PSL for me was like an aikido retreat. A phrase in many martial arts is "stepping onto the mat." It refers to willingly entering a specialized kind of activity designed to create personal feedback: to choose to engage in practice. Stepping onto the mat requires letting go of the safe critic's pose, to become the object of study. Before you enter the mat, there's no guarantee what you'll discover there. PSL is an opportunity, for a week, to step onto the mat, interacting with other professionals by mindfully solving problems that seem technical. With the talent available in a PSL workshop, the identified problem isn't the problem. How you go about solving it is the problem. The real practice in PSL isn't about using this communication model or that one; it is about choosing to practice awareness and reflection and choice in interactions with others. It's about bringing the clarity of the *dojo* floor to every interaction.

Another phrase from the martial ways is "training your stomach," using the words *hara* or *tanden*. *Hara* and *tanden* both refer to one's "center," located in the abdomen. "Center" is the place you live from, analogous to heart or head in the West. So "training your stomach" used this way is a sort of pun, meaning training the place you live from, which happens to be nearby. The training doesn't affect hunger so much as what you desire and the place of appetite in your life. Choosing in PSL is also a form of training your stomach, really training the center you live from. In PSL, you can choose to be receptive or not, to try a technique or not, to keep a journal or not, or even to show up for class or not. In the PSL *dojo*, there is no escaping questions about your own effectiveness and intention. How badly do you want to work better with others? What will you choose to do? Will you choose to observe or to participate? PSL is a week of choosing to practice techniques of interaction and observation. PSL is "training your stomach."

Immersive training in the martial arts is sometimes called *shugyo* ("shoe-geeoh," meaning "austere training," sometimes "forging"). *Shugyo* is choosing to step onto the mat exactly when there is every excuse not to: exhaustion, injury, too much information, fear. It has its rewards. Each hour, you learn more as experiences from the last hour inform this one. The lessons go deeper. They are more available when you need them. Merely choosing to step onto the mat one more time also teaches that you can choose. You can learn that practicing is a choice that is always available. The late aikido *Doshu* ("doe-shoe," for "head of the tradition"—the current head of a martial way) wrote that true aikido must become a lifestyle. I take that to mean in part that if you put the tools away when life gets rough, you haven't really learned much. The insights and models in aikido aren't just for the mat. Certainly not just to pass a test. PSL is like that.

That's all a little hard to remember while making the same stupid mistake for the fiftieth time. PSL was like that for me. Saying "not again" and getting up one more time, after a hard fall, to see if this time I could figure it out. Not using one of the models from PSL is as clear as the inability to move your hand an extra half inch, to turn your wrist a little more, to get it right when it matters. It is clear what disrupts your stance, what makes you literally lose your mind. It is also clear what is enough of an excuse for you to stop trying. PSL is about the habit of stepping onto the mat one more time, when you're sure you've had enough. PSL is about practicing new tools on an ongoing basis, not just learning new words or new moves. This is true of all the "ways" and of leadership.

I encountered aikido in a small article published in a free regional newspaper. When I called the *dojo*, the *sensei* ("sen-say," meaning "teacher") said, "Come and see." Immediately, I was facing a choice. If I didn't accept, why not? There was no special demonstration. We spoke a little, and I watched the class in silence. The next class began, and he said, "Come, and try it." And again, *Why not? What was I afraid of learning? What feedback from the training was such a risk? What was I afraid I might demonstrate, for myself and the world to see?* Of course, I was startled when I felt that first technique. I got thrown. My reaction was as plain there on the mat as a banner headline. Was my choice to embrace this, or reject it? Was my choice to learn how and why, or to avoid the situation and reject the experience? PSL is like that.

Eventually, being startled became a joy—at least some of the time—and I would laugh out loud, usually while four feet in the air. At one seminar, my training partner threw me into a wall. It was just a slip in concentration under the fatigue of several days' training. Smiling, Sugano-Sensei whispered "wall-*waza*" ("wah-zah," meaning "technique"). It was a sly joke. Encountering the wall let my partner experience his awareness of space and his management of the training itself. It allowed me to breakfall sideways. I hadn't known I could do that. It was another surprising chance to see *ai-ki-do*, "the blending energy way." You've got to blend with the unexpected wall, just as contracting gases need no permission. You don't get to choose the professional problems that present themselves, either. Leadership has got to be there when you need it. PSL is about that.

Although an injury (not related to aikido) has kept me from training, I continue to study aikido while working out so that I might be able to train again. I will find out whether this injury is an excuse or another startling encounter. I will find out how much I was able to translate from the mat to use when I need it. I'm not laughing about it yet. Leadership for me has a lot to do with time off for my body to heal, for one thing. Not that I'm happy about it, or that it is coming easily. But even an injury is an opportunity to practice aikido—and PSL—it turns out. PSL is about practicing awareness and reflection and choice in interactions under pressure. It is about the habit of leadership, practiced on the mat, where it is difficult to hide. It should probably be called PS-*do*, the problem-solving way.

You enter every experience with your intention and the tools you brought with you. You can choose how to be: how to act, whether to use the tools you have. You can choose to accept new information, new models, and new ways to interact, or not. Also whether to lead, or not. You can choose to see what is going on, or try to hide. You can choose to try something different. Some of the tools seem like magic. One taste and you want it all to be magic. Then you want to understand what is behind the magic. Getting what you glimpsed takes a lifetime. It is a practice—not a result. PSL is like that. Otherwise, it's just an enjoyable week with interesting people where you learn some things.

Aikido Sources
Morihei Uesheba created and headed aikido until his death in 1969. Aikido continued to grow under the guidance of his son, the late *Doshu*, Kisshomaru Uesheba, and many of the founder's students. Some of the founder's writings, and many of his son's, are readily available in English. Direct students whose work is also available in English include the Senseis: Yoshimitsu Yamada (New York), Mitsugi Saotome (San Diego), the late Gozo Shioda (Tokyo), Roy Suenaka (Charleston), Morihiro Saito (Tokyo), Ellis Amdur

(Seattle), and Gaku Homma (Denver). Probably still the best English-language student's introduction to aikido is Westbrook and Ratti's *Aikido and the Dynamic Sphere.*

Several American *aikidoka* have developed materials applying aikido principles off the mat. Among these are Tom Crum, Wendy Palmer, George Leonard, Richard Heckler, and the late Terry Dobson.

The late Donn F. Draeger's three-volume series, *The Martial Arts and Ways of Japan,* explores the evolution of the modern *do's* from the historical combative *jitsu's* in the context of Japan's history. Draeger-Sensei was one of the first Westerners to study and publish about martial arts in modern Japan. He held ranks in multiple modern and traditional arts, and was sponsor and mentor to many students who traveled to Japan to practice.

Aikido is certainly not the only martial way that uses practice and technique to teach awareness and self-mastery. The martial ways all address the same problem: people interacting and training to be responsible within the interaction. One of the best introductions to the martial ways is C.W. Nicol's *Moving Zen.* Nicol-Sensei practices and teaches Shotokan karate.

PSL Sources

Information on PSL is available on Jerry Weinberg's Website (www.geraldmweinberg.com). My PSL workshop faculty were Eileen Strider (www.striderandcline.com) and David Schmaltz (www.truenorth.com). The faculty for the other simultaneous session were Wayne Strider (www.striderandcline.com) and Naomi Karten (www.nkarten.com).

Like the community of martial artists, there is a community of software practitioners, teachers, and authors who mindfully practice systems development. The workshop called Problem Solving Leadership is one entry point to this community. Like aikido, the only way to really begin to understand is to try it.

11

The Consultant's Consultant

Tim Lister

I first met Jerry Weinberg's words during the winter of 1972-1973. I was a programmer in New York, having graduated from college the previous summer. I was writing assembly-language programs, and we had Michael Jackson, later to become the author of *Principles of Program Design*,[35] consult for our office. Under his direction, we built some control macros in order to write structured assembly-language programs using what came to be known as The Jackson Method. Life was really good, but being a 23-year-old at the time, I didn't understand. I thought that I was experiencing a typical life for a professional programmer. Only later in my career did I realize that I'd had the great good fortune of landing in an intellectual hotbed of software development.

One morning, my boss came out of her office (yes, "her"— she was a woman, and again, only later did I sadly realize what a rare place I inhabited). She was carrying two cardboard cartons. We gathered around her and could see that one carton was full of new engineering notebooks and the other was full of copies of a book, *The Psychology of Computer Programming,* by someone named Gerald M. Weinberg. She handed each of us one book from each carton and said, "Let's read this book together and talk about it as we go. You'll understand the notebooks once you get into the book."

With books in hand, off we went, back to our offices— remember walls that actually reached all the way up to the ceiling?—and back to work. I remember cracking open the Weinberg book on the subway. Once back at my apartment that night, I remember drinking a cold beer and reading on my sofa. The book was a pleasure to read, and, back at the office over the next few days, nobody was waiting for the boss to start the conversation. I remember all of us talking about what we would promise ourselves to log faithfully into our engineering diaries. There was very little balking, since it was clear to us that this Weinberg guy was the real deal. He was a programmer writing about what it was really like to work as a pro. Even though he was probably ancient—or so we imagined, given all the experience he seemed to have—he knew about our lives and our work. (I think Jerry was probably somewhere between thirty-five and forty when he wrote the book, but when you're twenty-three, that appears to be another generation. Over the years, our generations seem to have merged. How did that happen?)

Again, young and naive, I did not realize that Jerry was the first person to rightfully proclaim programming as an intensely human activity.

Over the years, Jerry wrote, and I read. Everyone probably has his own favorites, but mine are, in no particular order,

> *Are Your Lights On?* What is the problem, and who owns it?
>
> *Quality Software Management, Vols. 1–4:* Building a truthful, and therefore sustainable, management practice.
>
> *Exploring Requirements: Quality Before Design:* What do we want and need, not what we might think we want and need.
>
> *An Introduction to General Systems Thinking:* How systems work and change . . . really.
>
> *The Secrets of Consulting:* How to think about giving advice.

I think about how Jerry's words have changed my perceptions. I have become enormously skeptical of simple cause-and-effect explanations of any system behavior, such as, "They missed the project deadline because they weren't productive enough." I have lost trust in most correlations: "For the most difficult projects, you want the most experienced staff."

I have even changed my own definition of a system and its boundaries. For example, when Denver International Airport was built, among all the wonderful claims for it was the one that the airport would never close, even for a snowstorm. The advanced technology and machines would permit flights to take off and land even in the most adverse weather. Well, the first big snowstorm hit, and just about every flight got canceled. Why? It turns out that the pilots based in Denver (fairly wealthy folks) lived in the suburbs, up in the mountains, and they couldn't get themselves to the airport in the storm. The airport system was not bounded by its property.

And maybe most important of all (and I've been a consultant for about thirty years now), I thank Jerry for helping me think about system dynamics and change. In *The Secrets of Consulting*, Jerry points out, "Don't be rational, be reasonable." If logic always solved the problem, nobody would need a consultant. Having lived Jerry's advice for all these years, I'd like to add, "When the situation looks irrational and unreasonable, it isn't; you're just missing a key piece of the puzzle."

The following true story illustrates the wisdom in this particular piece of advice. What happened was a failure on my part. I was consulting at a company that had a large IT project just under way. I was coaching the team on getting a solid spec together, and at this point, I was coming in for a few days every few weeks. The project team had decided to deliver the system in three releases. The first would take about a year; the second, another eight or nine months. Full functionality would be with Release 3, about six months after Release 2.

We got to the point where we understood the requirements well enough that we could prioritize them with the stakeholders. I ambled into the office to start another visit and found a group of analysts waiting for me. The analysts all had one urgent complaint: The stakeholders were demanding that all the requirements be considered top priority—in effect, showstoppers. These requirements had to be in Release 1 or the release would be useless. The stakeholders refused to sign off unless they got their way.

I looked over some of the requirements, and they were clearly *not* showstoppers; they were mostly valuable, but not "must-haves." The analysts asked me to get this straightened out, the subtext being, "Please go knock their coconuts together until they come to their senses." I gathered some of the more obviously not-showstopper requirements and went out to meet the stakeholders to see what was up. This seemed so irrational, but could it be reasonable? What was I missing?

Sure enough, when I got to the stakeholders, they too were waiting to bend my ear. I began by showing them some of the requirements and stating that these were in no way showstoppers, according to the definition we had all agreed to. They looked at them and agreed that they weren't must-haves. I then said that the analysts had stated that the stakeholders wouldn't sign off unless these requirements were prioritized as must-haves. They said that was right, too: These requirements weren't showstoppers, but the stakeholders were indeed demanding that they be prioritized as such. With The Mad Hatter's Tea Party coming to my mind, I listened as they smiled ruefully and began to explain their rationale.

They had printed out some old project documents as evidence. It turns out that every time a project had been planned in releases, the same pattern unfolded. As they told it to me, the stakeholders and IT would expend blood, sweat, and tears to get Release 1 on the air. Once it stabilized, the stakeholders would turn to the team to say, "Let's get going on Release Two," but by then, most of the team had disappeared. The original team members had been reassigned to Release 1 of another project, so Release 2 would be badly understaffed. What was supposed to be an eight-month effort would end up as a fourteen-to-sixteen month slog. One stakeholder wistfully stated, "I've been here almost fifteen years, and I've never seen a Release Three."

It all made perfect sense. They didn't believe that their Release 2 was coming any time soon, and they believed that Release 3 was fiction. They were fighting to get as much into Release 1 as they could. They were hoping to pressure the project to add more people to deal with their one shot at getting as much of the functionality as they could. I told them that I understood and would get back to them soon.

I went back to the analysts, who were expecting me to tell them that I had snapped the stakeholders out of their dementia. I didn't know how to start, so I just said that it appeared they had trained the stakeholders really well. I went on to explain what I had learned, and I watched the analysts look at their shoes and admit that it was all too true. Since this was not an analysis problem, I went off to see the project manager.

The project manager seemed to be a very reasonable fellow; after all, he had hired me to consult. I relayed the news of the day to him, and he simply asked, "What do you think I should do?" I recommended that he personally promise the stakeholders that the project would end at Release 3, and that he would do his utmost to keep the team together through to the end. He looked at me and said, "I can't do that." I knew what he meant. Making those promises would put his career as a PM in jeopardy. It was not acceptable behavior for a PM in IT to make those promises. I said that it was entirely his call. He went to the analysts and told them to prioritize the requirements themselves, without seeking the stakeholders' approvals.

I knew the collegial spirit of the project had died. It was a sad day. The PM and I both knew that I could no longer be of any help. The whole story kept playing in my mind. What could I have done differently? I remembered Jerry's Hard Law from *Secrets of Consulting:* "If you can't accept failure, you'll never succeed as a consultant." But was there a solution out there? *Truly,* I thought, *What would Jerry have done and said? What is the real problem here?*

And then, suddenly, there it was in front of me. So simple. Release 3 should be named Release 1. The two releases prior to Release 1 could be given diminutive names like Interim A and Interim B, or Bridge 1 and Bridge 2. As long as the team declared the whole project one release, it could behave acceptably to the IT organization and get the job done for the stakeholders.

Even though the toothpaste was out of the tube, I e-mailed the PM with my solution for the next project. He wrote back, "That's crazy, but it just might work. How did you think of that?"

I wasn't on his payroll anymore, so I don't think I ever responded to him—until now: Jerry Weinberg taught me to think that way.

12

Writing Is the One Surefire Way to Avoid Writer's Block

Johanna Rothman

In his book on writing, Jerry Weinberg explains why there never needs to be such a thing as writer's block.[36] The antidote to writer's block is writing. When people experience what they claim is writer's block, it usually means they're trying to write about something they don't care about, or in a way that doesn't work for them. This is the essence of Weinberg's Writing Lesson Number One.[37]

One of the ways I've taught myself how to write differently is to remember how I used to write code or tests. A number of the approaches that used to help me see and solve hard technical problems also work for writing.

Write for a Limited Time

Timeboxing works for software development and testing, so don't be surprised that it works for writing. Although I prefer to set aside a few hours at a time to write, that only works when I know what I want to write about. If I don't quite know what I want to write or how to say it, I try some timed writing.

I start with five minutes. This small timebox helps me focus, and I know I don't have to stare for very long at a blank page, trying to figure out what to say. After five minutes, I may not have anything good, but I almost always generate some germ of an idea that I can use as I add to the piece or revise.

Timed writing works for me when the timeboxes are under twenty minutes. With more than twenty minutes, I procrastinate, checking my e-mail or reading a blog or writing something else.

Once you carve out a little something in a five-minute timebox, it helps you see the next little something, which makes the task (whether it's development, testing, or writing) much easier.

Write Something

During a writer's workshop led by Jerry, I learned how to use "blah blah blah." Writing something, even something as insignificant as "blah blah blah," makes me continue writing.

That may seem counterintuitive to you, but here's why it works for me: The blahs are boring. Since I normally combine the blahs with timeboxes, I don't want to stay bored for the entire five minutes—or worse, ten! Soon the ideas I'm trying to write about emerge. They don't emerge in final written form, but they do emerge. Once I have written something other than blahs, I can manage to edit and revise it as I proceed.

If you're a developer or tester, you can try this, too. You might not write "blah blah blah," but you can try something obvious. (When I develop code or tests, I generally timebox the obvious work.) Then ask yourself, What's another direction I might try, to find something interesting and not obvious?

Tell a Story

In software development and testing, reading other people's code and tests can sometimes provide you with one or two insights into what your code or tests might look like. Really great code or tests tell you a story about the problem the system is trying to solve. If I'm not sure how to get started, I try to think of telling a story first. The trick for me is to write a short story, just a paragraph or two that shows the problem I'm trying to write about.

Here's an example. In my forthcoming book about project portfolio management, I want to explain to senior managers that multitasking is evil, which is why they should use project portfolio management. I want them to feel the pain that developers and testers feel. Here's the (unedited) story I'm using to introduce the idea of evaluating all the projects against one another:

A Tale of Three Projects
by Hapless Developer

I'm sitting at my desk, completely stuck. I have three must-finish-now, ultra-high-crisis projects. Every time I start one, someone interrupts me with a question on one of the others. I can't escape anywhere—people have found me in the cafeteria, in the meeting room, in the lab. My manager came by yesterday morning to tell me the first project needs to be done now. Then he came by after lunch to tell me the second project needs to be done now. I stopped working on the first, and started on the second. Then he told me at the end of the day I need to finish the third.

I can't decide what to do first. What's the point of working on any one of these projects? He'll just come by and tell me to change before I finish anything. Maybe I'll work on my résumé or play a game of solitaire.

This is a first draft story, and may not sufficiently show the pain to managers. (I bet it does show the pain to technical contributors, however.)

How does a nonfiction writer learn to tell stories? By reading other writers closely. And by practicing writing of all kinds.

Practice Reading

Practicing reading may sound like a strange thing to tell someone who's trying to improve his or her writing skills, but it works. If you're trying to find your voice, read a few pages of a book or an article you really enjoy. Now take a five-minute timebox and analyze it. (No more than that, or you're escaping your writing. And we won't have that, will we?) What did you enjoy? It could be the plot, the characters, the description of the landscape, or the emotion in the story.

Once you can understand and articulate what you enjoy, you can practice writing something, using the piece you enjoyed as a model.

For example, I like reading breezy romance novels, science fiction (especially space operas), and murder mysteries. I might use the characterizations from one genre, or the plot devices of another genre, or the dialogue, or the plot twists. The dialogue helps me see how I want to tell the story. Serious science fiction tends to have specific good and evil forces, so the plot helps me think of the analogy in what I'm writing.

If you're a developer or tester, the best and fastest way to improve your code and tests is to read other people's code and tests. Reading with intention helps you see how other people solve specific problems—problems you might have at some point. And, as a writer, you'll find that the more you read other people's writing, the more options you have for how you might tell your stories.

Practice Writing

> *The more you write, the better your writing will be.* Really. Becoming a great writer is simple: You write, you edit, you ask for review, you edit some more, you get more reviews, and then you edit some more—until you're done. Only you know what "done" means, and this is different from software product development.
>
> The more you write, the better your writing will be. Start writing now.

The more you read, the better your writing will be. And the more you practice writing, the better your writing will be. If you haven't yet started a journal or a blog—even a private blog—start. The discipline of writing several times a week for publication will force you to write smaller pieces, pieces that can grow up to be longer pieces. When you're stuck, you can take one of those small pieces and make it bigger. You probably won't just make it longer. When I start with a blog entry, I tend to treat it as the middle of a piece and expand it from there.

You may be shaking your head, thinking, *Oh, Johanna's gone off the deep end again.* You may even suspect that this approach may work for fiction writers but wonder how it can possibly work for nonfiction writers. *Besides, I'm not a writer, I just want to write better reports.*

Talk About Your Topic

If you're an extrovert like me, be careful not to talk too much about your topic. Otherwise, you'll talk the writing away. But if you're stuck, take a short timebox, find a sympathetic ear, and talk through the angle you need to take on the writing you're trying to start or finish.

I find that if I talk for more than ten minutes to my sympathetic ear, I may talk away the piece and lose interest in writing it. I need just enough talk time to get started and no more. When I was new to writing for a professional audience, I sometimes needed five minutes to get started and another five minutes in the middle.

When I was a developer, I needed to talk through many of my problems before I could finalize the code. I pretended I was discussing the requirements or the design, but I was really talking through the problems. As a tester, I talked through the problems with the developers before I started testing, or sometimes during testing. One of my favorite tactics was to have lunch with the developers

I'm not a writer, or am I? you wonder. In truth, you are both a nonfiction and a fiction writer. Every writer has elements of fiction—even if you just change the names to protect the guilty. Every writer has elements of nonfiction—even if it's just the data. Think about writing use cases, user stories, or defining personas. Are requirements fiction or nonfiction? I assert they are both—fiction before the product is developed, and nonfiction afterward. Software developers write about their code, especially in comments. Testers write about their tests, especially in defect reports. The better you are as a writer, the better your requirements, code, and tests will be.

You are a writer. You might not have enough experience to be a facile writer, but you are a writer.

and ask, "Where in this module were you challenged or surprised?" I didn't ask what was hard; too many developers can't admit that anything about their code was hard. But developers like explaining the challenges and how they solve those challenges. By hearing about their challenges, I had new avenues to consider for testing. I would never have thought about those problems without talking through them as a developer or as a tester, because I need to talk in order to think.

Start Where You Are

Just as I advise people and organizations to start change from wherever they are, I advise writers to start writing with the most compelling part of what they're writing. For many people, that's not the beginning.

Maybe you have a great summary line. Wonderful! Write that down. Now, ask yourself what you would have to write to make the truth of that summary line clear to others. (Yes, this is test-driven writing.)

Test-driven development and test-driven test development both start with answers to a question: What would the system have to do to create this outcome? As you write, use a form of that question—What would I have to say to get people to react in this way?—and you'll have a way to start.

The key with writing is to start somewhere. It doesn't matter where, because you'll have to edit and revise the writing anyway. So, start somewhere you have energy, and you'll be able to start and revise as you need.

Avoid the Title Trap

I find titles the hardest part of writing. And I still practice titling every chance I get. For me, that means generating several titles. For example, this essay has had several titles:

In Defense of Practice

Writing Is All About Avoiding Writer's Block

Maybe Writing Is Just Like Software Development

Writing Is the Way to Avoid Writer's Block
Becoming a Better Writer

You can see elements of all those titles in this essay. I probably evolved several more titles before I decided on the final title. And, once I turn a piece over to the editors, they usually help me refine the title. Once I do have the final title, I make another pass through the text to make sure all the text still hangs together with that title.

Titles can create writer's block. Don't let your title force you to write in one direction—your brain might want to take you in another direction. Use a title as a guideline, not as a definitive path to the piece. I let my subconscious brain take over when I write. If you realize you have to write something else before you can write about the topic you're supposed to address, write that down. Save it. Now you've freed your mind to think about the topic at hand.

Pair–Write

Pairing, the way two developers write the same piece of code in front of one computer with one keyboard, is another option if I'm stuck. Pairing works very well for developing and testing. Once I got over issues with my ego, I found pairing as a developer to be highly productive. And pairing as a tester helped me see other potential areas to test much faster than if I'd worked alone.

But pairing as a writer is a little different. When people pair-write code or tests, they have a finite number of possible statements. But pairing to write in natural language is harder because there is no single reasonable way to approach the writing problem, certainly no One Right Way. But if you're really stuck, pair-writing works.

Pair-writing works because you first have to discuss the problem with the other part of your pair. With the discussion, you flesh out the problems you want to solve with your writing and define how you might want to start. When I pair-write with Esther Derby, one of my coauthors, we talk about the situation and about how we want to introduce the situation, and then we take off from there. We don't start with much detail, but we write a bit, talk a bit, write a bit, and continue. With another coauthor, Joe Rainsberger, we draw pictures and generate an outline. We don't necessarily stick with the whole outline, but we've discussed the problem in detail.

Use Inspections and Reviews

One of my approaches is to write until I can't figure out what else to say. I generally send the writing out for review and ask my reviewers, "What else do you want to know from this piece?" Some people provide a substantial, detailed review, more like an inspection. Some people provide a meta-review, perhaps saying, "I enjoyed it up until here, and then you lost me." Some people provide a list of opportunities to add details in specific areas.

Inspections and reviews of writing work the same way they do for code and tests. The more comfortable you are with peer reviews of your technical work, the more comfortable you'll be with peer reviews of your writing—and the better you will write.

Put Your Writing Away for a Few Days

Sometimes, you write for a while and then get stuck. You may be stuck because you need to eat or sleep. Or, you may have run out of ideas *for now.* I find that if I write a bunch of different pieces during the day, I run out of ideas late in the afternoon.

As with development and testing, putting away your writing for a few days lets you think about it subconsciously. The more you let your subconscious mind think about what you're writing, the more flexible, adaptable, and just plain interesting ideas you'll be likely to surface.

Write Differently Than You Prefer

Everyone has a default approach to writing. Some of us like to start at the beginning and work our way down to the end. Some people like to make an outline. Some people start with mind maps and write pieces, seeing how the whole work comes together. Some people have a germ of an idea and write around it, spiraling in and out until the work is done.

When you're stuck, try another way. Since I'm a top-down person, my next approach is to try an outline. If an outline doesn't work, I'll take the time and mind-map or draw a picture of the situation I'm trying to describe.

What's key is to try something different. I've done this as a developer, too. One time, I was developing test code for a process control system, but I was stuck on how to test a certain piece of it. I realized that a diagram of the piece of the system, combined with a mind map, might give me another approach to the test development. It did, and completely changed *and simplified* my testing approach.

When Nothing Works

Sometimes, you try all these things, and you still don't discover the flow of writing the piece. Then it's time to do something completely different, away from your writing.[38] I find physical activity, such as walking, working out, or practicing shooting baskets works best for me. Some people find that working with their hands, perhaps doing crafts, works best for them.

The reason these activities work is that doing something completely different prompts you to come at the problem from a different direction. You might come up with a different angle on the piece, or a different start, or a different end.

All of the Above

All of these ideas work. Some of them will work for you better than others. In fact, I have a confession: I was stuck on how to start, edit, and finish this essay, so I followed all the suggestions I've covered. With any luck, you will rarely use all of them for one work, but isn't it nice to know you could?

13

Generational Systems Thinking

Jonathan Kohl

Sometimes, people from earlier generations are surprised that I count Jerry Weinberg as an influence. They are even more surprised by the degree to which Jerry's work influences mine. Once, during a meeting with a potential client, I mentioned an idea I'd derived from Jerry. One of the managers looked shocked and then said, "No offense, but I was very surprised to hear someone from your generation talk about that. I haven't heard that idea in years." Something important had occurred at that moment. The tone of the meeting changed, and we now had a shared point of contact. Later conversations and interactions built on that shared knowledge of Jerry's work. We discovered that we had a lot more in common than we initially thought.

I may be a Weinberg-influenced, born-in-the-seventies Generation-Xer in the software community, but I am hardly an anomaly. I recently polled some friends from my generation and asked them if they had also discovered Jerry's work. I heard a range of answers from: "Yes, I've heard of him and seem to remember reading something by him, but don't remember much now," to "Oh yeah, I read *The Psychology of Computer Programming* in university and it was great," to "I heard about him years ago, read his work, and posted some of his quotations on the wall at my first job," to people who have not only read Jerry's work, but have met and interacted with Jerry at conferences and workshops.

One of my friends and colleagues, Aaron West, described a common path of discovery. He began reading about Jerry online (in his case, on the famous C2 wiki). He later found a copy of one of Jerry's books, and went on to read it and several others. Aaron eventually attended workshops with Jerry, learning from him in person. Jerry's work is alive and well in my and younger generations.

Recently, I worked at a software start-up with one of my coworkers, also a "born in the seventies" consultant who has been influenced by Jerry's work. We were discussing a difficult challenge, and he asked, "Do you think the Satir communication-stances model would be helpful to consider at this point?" I was surprised to hear someone else mention a powerful model that helps identify and effectively deal with unhealthy communication situations. We had both learned about this from Jerry's work, where he applied these kinds of models to software teams.[39]

Using this model, my colleague and I managed to navigate our way through a difficult communication issue. We discovered that we hadn't been communicating in a way that management could identify with. In short order, we adapted our communication-style methods and had much better success. Drawing on Jerry's work helped us come up with a solution much more quickly than merely brainstorming and using a trial-and-error approach.

When I think about how I discovered Jerry's work, I struggle to pinpoint just one source. Jerry's name had mind-share with me, even before my colleagues and mentors encouraged me to delve more deeply into his work. I think my familiarity with his work was due to it being cited so often by a wide variety of people in the software development world. I also found that many of the influential people whose work I read early in my career cited Jerry. James Bach quotes Jerry a good deal, for example, and others, such as Michael Bolton, might preface an answer to a question with a quotation from Jerry. I remember starting to read whatever I could find of Jerry's work online, at the urging of my friend and colleague Chris Stott. For several years, Chris had been a staff consultant with one of the largest consultancies in the world; after that, he was a senior manager and eventually an independent consultant. I was wrestling with the decision over whether to become an independent consultant, and Chris answered, "Read Jerry Weinberg's work!" I did. And I profited from it.

Soon after talking with Chris, I met Sherry Heinze at a conference. Sherry does work as a software testing contractor, so we had a lot to talk about. We started out talking in a hallway for quite a while, and, realizing it was past noon, decided to continue the conversation over lunch. At the end of the meal, Sherry looked at me with a sidelong glance and said, "You think about things differently. You need to get more involved with Jerry Weinberg's work." At that point, I decided to immerse myself, sometimes reading two or three of his books at the same time.

When I ask others about how Jerry's work came to be a frequent source of inspiration for them, they have similar stories. Others have mentioned that Jerry's name seemed familiar, and one day they saw a copy of *The Psychology of Computer Programming* or a volume of *Quality Software Management* in their workplace, borrowed it, read it, and found it changed their thinking about software. Others mention hearing someone cite Jerry's work, which was enough to tip the scales for them to investigate further. Each person I've talked to has commented that Jerry's work had a significant impact on the way he or she thinks about working on software development projects.

Jerry has had an impact on my work in several ways. One of the most obvious is in the way I think about the social and relationship implications of software development. When I was in university, I worked a variety of different jobs to pay my way. I mostly worked as a salesman, and later on, as a waiter in a popular local restaurant. In both jobs, relationships with people were incredibly important, and I succeeded because I understood that. Somehow, I forgot about this when I started developing software systems. In the technology industry, we spend so much time trying to control machines that we start thinking like machines. Thinking that way is clear cut: Our software program either works or doesn't work; our code either compiles or doesn't compile. However, because programming-related tasks are so labor-intensive, we get obsessed with the machine, and forget *whom* the machine serves. A computer has no emotions, but we as humans are a tangle of emotions. Emotions are an integral part of our makeup, and they drive most of what we do in life. Jerry's work reminded me to focus once again on what was really important: the people. Jerry also taught me how to view people as *part* of a complex, interrelated system.

As new generations emerge and find their way in the software industry, many do as I did: Seek out those who have come before, for guidance and advice. In my generation, we have looked

to influential people including Steve McConnell (software development thinker and author of the now classic *Code Complete*),[40] Joel
Spolsky (author and blogger on software development issues),[41]
Kent Beck (one of the founders of the software development
process Extreme Programming),[42] and James Bach (software
testing consultant, author, and speaker).[43] Tellingly, all these
people mention Jerry's work or cite him as an influence. A more
recent influential figure in the software development community is
the twenty-something software developer David Heinemeier
Hansson, creator of the wildly popular Web application development framework Ruby on Rails. David also mentions Jerry in his
work.[44]

I asked David how he discovered Jerry's work, how it had
influenced him, and if he recommends Jerry's work to others.
David replied, "It seems that all roads lead to Jerry, so it's hard to
pinpoint exactly what led to my first discovery of him. But I
remember the first book of Jerry's I got was *Secrets of Consulting*.
That was all it took to get me hooked on his amazing writing skills
and insight." David points to Jerry's adaptation of the Satir model
of congruent communication as a major influence: "My favorite
Jerry word is 'congruence.' I never thought about it so explicitly
before Jerry introduced it to me. That's probably one of the biggest
impacts I've felt. That, and his focus on restating problems. While
the former has made me a better coworker, the latter has made me
a much better programmer." David says he tries to recommend
Jerry's work to others: "Especially short books like *Are Your Lights
On?* which are easy ways of getting into his work. I also no longer
have my own copy of *Secrets of Consulting*, after having loaned it
out repeatedly."[45] David's story sounds familiar. Since influential
thinkers mention Jerry, those who are influenced by them are also
turned on to his work.

As I look at what's on my desk, amid piles of papers, a cell
phone, an Apple iPod, a laptop, and other devices, I see several
technical books—on software testing, Ruby (a scripting language),
Java (a popular programming language developed by Sun
Microsystems), C# (a popular programming language developed
by Microsoft), and Ruby on Rails. But then there's *An Introduction
to General Systems Thinking*. Why, amid the current technology
books, mostly published within the last two years, do I have a book

that is almost as old as I am? Because much of Jerry's work transcends eras, it has an almost universal applicability. For example, I use *An Introduction to General Systems Thinking* so frequently—both as a reference and as a tool to help expand my thinking—that it rarely moves off my desk onto my pile of books on the floor or my bookshelf. That explains the rough appearance, dog-eared pages, and different colors of pen or highlighter used throughout. As an exercise, I let the pages fall open to the spot where the book would most naturally open, where the spine is the weakest. Doing this exercise recently, I came across this section on page 52, highlighted in blue: "What is a system? As any poet knows, *a system is a way of looking at the world.*"

This is a powerful insight and a great thinking tool. As a consultant working in technology, I find being able to look at systems from different perspectives incredibly useful. I aim to see things from different perspectives, because when I do, important insights that help guide my work frequently occur to me. In my consulting work, I am often called in to help teams solve a difficult problem. Helping them look at their problem from different perspectives is often enough for them to figure out how to solve it.

When I give a talk or write an article, I know I've hit the mark if Sherry Heinze asks, "How did you get so smart so fast?" According to Sherry, Jerry wrote "How did you get so smart so fast?" in response to an idea I brought up on an online forum. Of course, I didn't "get smart" quickly. What I've done is look to those who came before me and work hard to understand the lessons they already learned. Recently, as an outspoken practitioner and critic of the popular Agile software development process movement, I've been asked to weigh in on process work. Without fail, when I think I have discovered some important, unique insight, all I have to do is look to Jerry's work and realize that thirty or forty years ago, Jerry had similar insight. In an industry that glorifies change, youthfulness, and newness, we frequently forget to look at the lessons from the past. Jerry's work is a gold mine of lessons from which future generations could spend years learning. Since Jerry has published many of his ideas, I have the luxury of time to learn and apply them in my own work. More importantly, I get to use Jerry's ideas to complement my own as I work with others.

Jerry's work has influenced many areas of my work. As I've mentioned, *An Introduction to General Systems Thinking* is a valuable resource for me because I am a professional who gets paid to help solve problems. Jerry's four *Quality Software Management* volumes are full of insights for me, particularly as a software tester who cares about quality. *The Secrets of Consulting* and *More Secrets of Consulting* are constant resources for me in my role as an independent consultant. I frequently consult *Exploring Requirements: Quality Before Design,* which Jerry coauthored with Don Gause, when working with the people who pay us technologists to help them solve their business problems. Jerry's *Weinberg on Writing: The Fieldstone Method* is useful for me as an author, as I try to wire together my thoughts into something readers might enjoy. As I read more of Jerry's body of work, I discover more insights and areas to apply them. I also pass those on to others that I work with. My copies of Jerry's books are frequently loaned out or given away to colleagues.

One client brought me in to audit its software development practices and to provide mentoring and training for the software testing group. All of the testers were under the age of thirty and brought energy and exuberance to the project. It was energizing to work with them—there was no problem that they deemed too large or too difficult, and they were filled with optimism. The test manager asked me to meet with the team alone, away from her influence, so I could get a more accurate picture of issues the testers struggled with.

In the meeting, one of the testers expressed a problem while the rest of the team nodded along vigorously: "We are often on very tight deadlines, and no one on the team, including us, has enough time to spend on a project," she said. "After the product goes out the door, there are almost always problems. As testers, we get blamed for not finding the problems before the software shipped. How do you deal with getting blamed all the time?"

"I don't accept the blame," I responded. "I refuse to play along in a blame game. If I don't accept the blame, what happens to it?"

I saw a flash in her eyes. She seemed to understand immediately what I meant, without elaboration. Even so, I explained what I meant by drawing on Jerry's work, describing the Satir communication-stances model, and how to be congruent in communication (say what you mean, and take yourself, others, and the context into account). That flash told me that I had introduced her to a different way of thinking. I could almost see a lightbulb turn on over her head, like they do in cartoons. After that meeting, some of my "Jerry books" were borrowed by some of the team members.

Jerry's work is one example of what Malcolm Gladwell defines in *The Tipping Point* as "sticky."[46] This means that certain ideas tend to persist, or cling to our consciousness. A sticky idea is easily understood and remembered. Jerry's ideas stick with me for several reasons. One is his humility, which carries an urge to improve and learn more. On the first page of *An Introduction to General Systems Thinking,* Jerry reflects on how little we really know about the world, with this statement: "The first step to knowledge is the confession of ignorance. We know far, far less about our world than most of us care to confess. Yet confess we must, for the evidences of our ignorance are beginning to mount, and their scale is too large to be ignored!" That is a statement I can identify with, and it is encouraging coming from someone with so many years of experience. That expression of humility is something that sticks with me and reminds me to keep striving to learn more.

Jerry has a brilliant way of expressing ideas memorably. A word that pops up in Jerry's work sometimes is *heuristic,* which he defines as a potentially helpful but non-guaranteed method for approaching the solution to a problem.[47] *Heuristic* is a word that makes people nervous. Maybe it seems big and confusing and academic, or they spelled it wrong in their fourth grade spelling bee and have harbored resentment over it ever since. It's too bad they get caught up on the word, because it is a powerful concept that is incredibly useful in our ever-changing environment.

Law is also a word that can make people nervous, but it carries an authority that gets our attention. By combining a word like *law* with something innocuous like *jam* or *jelly,* Jerry disarms the "one-true-way" dictum a law implies. The inherent stickiness of *jam* aside, this is a clever way to make an idea memorable. Jerry reminds us through his many "laws" that our methods for solving problems can have unexpected results. Through his use of language and ideas, he *demonstrates* heuristics. We get the point without having to grapple with the concept of heuristics itself.

One of my favorites is The Law of Raspberry Jam: "The wider you spread it, the thinner it gets."[48] Sometimes, when I do a talk and end up clarifying some points afterward, one-on-one with some audience members, I feel disappointed that the ideas I expressed during the talk didn't get through as clearly to the crowd as they did later, one-on-one. I need only remember The Law of Raspberry Jam to feel reassured, realizing that Jerry experienced the same problem I did, many years before.

Jerry's most popular and enduring work addresses the intersection of humans and computers and the social issues we deal with in those situations. Technology comes and goes, but we remain emotionally driven creatures who engage in complex relationships as we try to accomplish goals while working together. Software development projects are no exception to these dynamics.

This summer, a friend and band member from my university days came through town. Jim was a fabulous lead guitarist in various incarnations of what we called The Band back in university. At home on weekends, now, he is a lead guitarist in a local band. During the week, he earns his living as a manager in a transport truck sales and service company. Jim manages salespeople, mechanics, other managers, and people in many other roles. He is a few years older than me, and I sometimes seek his advice. When Jim and I last talked about leadership, he said, "You know, there is no technical problem that you can't solve if you have the right people on your team. The hard problems are the people problems. Managing *those* is the most important lesson I have learned. Those are the issues that they don't teach us in technical schools." I immediately thought of Jerry's work and felt grateful that I have it to draw on, as I navigate these kinds of challenges in my own work. Jim doesn't have a leader like that in his field. I have Jerry and those influenced by Jerry. We are fortunate that Jerry has been so willing to share his insights with those who come after him.

I'm certain that in years to come when my Java, Ruby on Rails, and .NET books have been replaced by the next popular programming technology books, *An Introduction to General Systems Thinking, Becoming a Technical Leader,* the *Quality Software Management* series, and Jerry's other books will still enjoy positions of prominence in my library. As I gain more experience, I find that, like others before me, I recommend and share Jerry's work with those who are coming into the industry after me. Thanks to Jerry's body of work, many of us from different generations and walks of life share similar ways of looking at the world. His ideas are part of the glue that binds us together.

14

Living in a Dream World

Dani Weinberg

"It won't last," said the jeweler who sold us my wedding ring. He was talking about the ring—a very narrow strip of gold—and he was right. Forty-three years later, my finger and knuckle had swollen alarmingly, and we thought we'd better remove the ring before it killed me. Jerry actually had to cut it off, and I got to pick out a new one in a larger size.

But the jeweler wasn't the only one, those many years ago, who said "It won't last." The others were referring to the marriage. People warned me, sometimes tried to frighten me, that I was making a huge mistake marrying this strange fellow. As the years went by and the mistake had not yet manifested itself, those people said that we were living in a dream world, a fantasy. Why else would we believe that we had a wonderful marriage?

Our response (just between the two of us) was: Great! Let's continue living in our dream world!

As I thought about writing this essay, I wondered how I could possibly write about our working partnership without also talking about our personal partnership. As many couples who work together know, these are really inseparable. Finally, I admitted to myself that I couldn't separate the two. So what you'll read about here is the dream world in which Jerry and I have been living for the past forty-six years.

I tried to recall our first experience of working together. I couldn't. That worried me a little. Was this a sign of early dementia? Or an indication that our earliest years working together were not memorable, maybe even very forgettable? I finally understood why I couldn't remember. In our forty-six years together, we have each reinvented ourselves several times, and we've also—necessarily—reinvented our personal and working relationships.

All well and good, but how am I going to get that information back again, now that it's lost somewhere in our former lives? I decided to dig out my curriculum vitae from my anthropology (pre-dog-training) days. It turned out that this was possibly the best reason to keep a CV on file: to explore the past. I was amazed at what I saw.

Our relationship over the years has been a rich, colorful fabric, consisting of our separate careers and their frequent meshing. In and out of the pattern each of us moved, sometimes separately, creating our own individual patterns, sometimes together. In some places, the fabric is smooth. In others, it's worn and frayed—not so much showing age as pressures from life.

From the CV, I also noticed that the weaving and interweaving were closely tied to geographic locations. Not surprising for an IBM ("I've Been Moved") couple, as we were in our first years together. And not surprising for the academic couple we soon became. And not surprising for a couple sharing an independent consulting practice, as we emerged.

As I sorted through my CV and my memory, I realized that our "working together" was perhaps not always visible to people outside our dream world. In addition to our obvious partnerships in teaching workshops and consulting to organizations, we've been partners from the very beginning. As in any productive partnership, we've collaborated on a variety of projects—some "his" and some "hers" and some "ours." And, as in any well-functioning partnership, we've provided each other with support and resistance, as appropriate. We've shared successes and failures. We've survived dysfunctional experiences. And—oh, yes—we even renamed our business once. About the only partnership kind of thing we've never quite gotten around to doing is creating a brochure (though we did once get as far as trying to design one). But there's still time!

New York City and Ann Arbor

Our first ten years together were spent doing what many couples do in their twenties. We were learning how to be married, continuing our educations, and starting our professional lives.

Jerry was already an experienced husband, having been married before, and his professional career was already well started. When we met, he had completed his work on Project Mercury in Washington, D.C., and was now teaching at the IBM Systems Research Institute in New York City.

I was still trying to figure out what I wanted to be when I grew up. I had graduated from college a music major, intending to be a concert pianist. Then, deciding that was unrealistic, I went to graduate school in musicology for a numbing three years and a master's degree. After all that, I couldn't find any work in my field except for giving piano lessons at a local settlement house. It's worth mentioning that during my vision quest for a career, I actually applied to IBM to be a systems service rep (Jerry insists they were called girls and not reps). Fortunately, IBM decided it didn't need to hire any more people that year.

Finally, I gave up on music and did what many young women my age were doing. I found an "interesting," low-paying job that I really enjoyed, working for the Junior Red Cross.

About a year into our marriage, IBM awarded Jerry a Resident Study Fellowship to go back to school—anywhere, in any field, all expenses paid. He already had a master's degree in physics. He had dropped out of the Ph.D. program at the University of California at Berkeley so that he could work for IBM, doing what he'd dreamed of since he was eleven years old—working with computers.

With Jerry's fellowship in our future, I, too, began to have an appetite for a doctorate, but with no particular field of study in mind. After enrolling and almost immediately dropping out of a doctoral program in music education (following just the first meeting of the first course), I participated in what might be considered Jerry's and my first experience of working together: a career counseling session in our VW bug as Jerry and I drove to D.C. to visit his kids. As we turned onto Constitution Avenue, Jerry summarized the session by saying, "I think you want to be an anthropologist"—to which I responded, "What's that?"

We spent the next three years as nontraditional (that is, *over-privileged*) graduate students at the University of Michigan, in Ann Arbor. Jerry wrote "Experiments in Problem Solving" as his Ph.D. dissertation in the communications sciences program. I was one of his anonymous, experimental subjects. The dissertation is probably Jerry's only nonfiction work that has never been published, though you can now find it on the Web, thanks to James Bach. (Go to Jerry's Website, geraldmweinberg.com, and look under "Jerry's early books.")

At Jerry's urging, I published my first significant anthropological study, "Models of Southern Kwakiutl Social Organization," in the journal *General Systems.* Little did I know that Jerry and I would coauthor a book about general systems thinking, fourteen years later. Eventually titled *General Principles of Systems Design,* the book brought together our work in technology (Jerry's side) and culture (my side). So the Kwakiutl provided the seed that would later germinate and grow into our collaboration as writers.

We left Ann Arbor three years later with a Ph.D. for Jerry and a second M.A. for me. We still had strong ties to New York City and returned to live there for the next two years. Jerry was back at the Systems Research Institute, and I was teaching anthropology at Hunter College and preparing for my Ph.D. preliminary exams at Michigan.

During that period, I got to see an unfamiliar side of my husband when we went to a Project Mercury reunion dinner. The reunion was held in the ballroom of one of the big hotels in the city. Over Peach Melba, various project members got up and spoke. All I remember—and very vividly—was seeing this gentle, tender man who was my husband stand up and sound like a hard-nosed, cerebral, witty project manager—which is, of course, what he had been just a few years before. People found his comments hilarious. I had no idea what he was talking about. As the years went by, I learned to enjoy his war stories as much as anyone else and even learned to speak the language well enough to communicate effectively with our clients. That's what being an anthropologist will do for you!

Fortunately, Jerry acknowledged the existence of people and feelings in this world, and I came to appreciate and even indulge in analytical thinking. A few years later, we had learned how to meld our styles to become an effective consulting team.

Switzerland

I passed my prelims, resigned from my job at Hunter, and was ready to do fieldwork for my dissertation. I had taken my exams on the geographic area of New Guinea, and that was where I wanted to go. My grant application to the NIH was awarded, but it was a dry grant—all the honor and no money. As explaind to me by an insider, NIH was just not giving money to married women because their husbands could pay for their fieldwork—a bit of a problem.

And then another problem surfaced. My advisor informed me that malaria was endemic in the Western Pacific and elephantiasis in the Eastern Pacific. Some choice. Jerry and I had planned to go together, wherever I needed to locate, but Jerry's health history precluded either of these possibilities.

As we were mulling all of this over, IBM invited Jerry to be the sole American faculty member at its new European Systems Research Institute, which happened to be not in Port Moresby, New Guinea, but in Geneva, Switzerland. My wise husband suggested that this might be just the right solution for us: He could work in Geneva while I did my field research somewhere in the Swiss Alps. Having set my stomach for New Guinea, though, the idea of studying Swiss peasants did not appeal to me. I dutifully went to see a professor of mine whose specialty was European peasantry, and he assured me that there was a lot to do there. So, off we went.

We moved to Geneva in 1967, and I found what seemed like the right mountain village to study. For the next two years, I lived in the village, and Jerry came up to spend weekends with me. Not content to be just "Madame's husband," he set himself the task of writing a computer program to do genealogical analysis for me. Every Sunday night, I'd send him back to Geneva with assorted scraps of paper on which I had collected information about who was who, who the ancestors were, who was married to whom. Every Friday night, Jerry made the trip back from the big city to my mountain village, lugging several pounds of computer printout in his backpack. (Remember that this was before the personal computer, so all this was done on mainframes.)

Out of this professional collaboration, rough-hewn as it was, came several papers that we each presented at our respective professional conferences—his about the software, and mine about the villagers and their social connections. An important part of my dissertation and my future publications would not have been possible without Jerry's technical collaboration.

Occasionally, I was invited to participate in ethnology symposia at the university in Geneva, and Jerry happily sat in the audience as the husband. This fit very nicely with the Swiss cultural view that women, though not allowed to vote or hold office at the federal level until 1971, were now accepted as professionals in their own right. This change was just one of many reasons we fell in love with Switzerland. We dreamed of being offered honorary citizenships (something almost impossible to come by unless your mother was a citizen) and spending the rest of our lives in that wonderful country.

Instead, we moved to Binghamton, New York.

We arranged to make the move over a period of a few months, during which we drove from Switzerland all the way through Italy. Typical of Weinberg and Weinberg "vacations," we worked as we traveled—Jerry wrote the full first draft of *The Psychology of Computer Programming,* and I wrote most of my dissertation on that trip. Jerry worked on an Olivetti portable typewriter; I wrote by hand. (Ah, the bad old days!)

Had my husband not given me the proverbial kick in the pants, I might still be writing my dissertation. While he typed away in one hotel room after another, I worried the time away trying to decide how to start writing. Finally, one day, Jerry said the words that I've since heard him say to many young writers: "Just start anywhere. You don't have to start at the beginning." Out of that kick came the first words of Chapter 4: "Two hundred and fifty people live in Bruson. . . ." And then the rest began to flow.

Binghamton and Lincoln

Once again, we were in a transitional period. For the first three years, we both lived in Binghamton. Jerry was one of the founding faculty of the School of Advanced Technology at the State University of New York, and I was a very junior member of the Anthropology department faculty. Jerry found several kindred spirits there, and together they created Ethnotech, the predecessor of Weinberg and Weinberg. I was winning a strong following of students while getting increasingly unpleasant vibes from my department chair. In spite of that, however, I led anthropological field schools in Europe every summer, with Jerry by my side. We were also co-faculty in an experimental program for freshmen called the Integrated Semester. We both still hear from our students from those days.

Three years later, I'd had enough of Binghamton and my faculty colleagues. Jerry and I talked about how I might find another job. I ran a "position wanted" ad in a professional newsletter, and Jerry made sure I included this sentence: "If you're just looking to fill a slot, please do not reply." After a few misadventures—such as going to one university interview not knowing I was the token woman candidate—I got the reply I was hoping for. It came from the department chair at the University of Nebraska-Lincoln. I went there for an interview, loved the department, and came home full of hope and excitement.

Jerry had said he'd follow me wherever I wanted to go, and I'm sure he meant it. I'm also sure he never imagined I'd want to move to Nebraska. He had gone to school in Omaha and Lincoln, and his parents still lived in Omaha, as well as many of his relatives. Years later, he confessed this was a difficult move for him. His relationships with his family had always been strained, and it worried him to be so close to them again. But at the time, he never said a word about this, fearing I would give up my dream. Those few years were not very pleasant on the home front as he tried hard to hide his disappointment and support me at all costs. Is that what partners should do? Absolutely not. We learned that lesson the hard way.

So, while I began teaching at UNL and having my most productive research and publishing years since starting out in anthropology, Jerry remained in Binghamton, supporting his colleagues and graduate students for a little while longer. Once a month, he came to Lincoln to spend a weekend with me. We had what is now called a commuting marriage, but at the time, that kind of relationship was nameless and simply unconventional—and, I might add, probably as difficult as it is now.

Finally, two years later, I was awarded tenure and Jerry left Binghamton to live in Lincoln with me. We bought a house in the country, a few miles outside of town. It came with cats: three litter-mates who lived in the garage and slept in our basement. Our first dog came into our life that winter, and others soon followed, fore-shadowing yet another pattern that would be woven into the fabric of our partnership.

Our second year together in Lincoln marked the beginning of our visible working partnership. Jerry and I spent many happy hours with Don Gause designing a five-day residential workshop that we were to teach that summer of 1974, in Australia. I distinctly remember us playing with tissues, trying to find ways to solve one of the problems we had designed for the workshop. We had identified an audience for the workshop that we called tech-nical leaders, and this workshop would help them go beyond their technical skills into the more difficult human issues involved in software development. We called this the Technical Leadership Workshop. TLW gradually evolved into PSL, our Problem Solving Leadership workshop.

As PSL evolved—and as Jerry and I evolved—it would increasingly deal with the people issues in any workplace or enter-prise. We wanted the workshop to have near-universal value, and we took great joy in the fact that our students were not only computing people but also dentists, psychotherapists, nurses, architects, teachers, organization development professionals, and even anthropologists.

We taught PSL together for many years, sometimes joined by a third colleague or an apprentice. We offered PSL as a public workshop and also as part of our consulting process with many technical organizations. We saw ourselves as change agents working from within organizations, and sometimes we helped our clients develop their own "change artists."

Every morning, when I wake up, I have the pleasure of looking at a quilt that some of those change artists made for us. It's hanging on our bedroom wall. The participants each contributed a square that expressed some important learning or experience that came out of our relationship with them. Sometimes I imagine those quilt squares sewn not onto a solid black background but overlaid on the complex fabric that is Weinberg and Weinberg. The colors might clash in a few places, and the background might become foreground in others, but what a vital and dynamic work of art that would be!

During those PSL years, I continued my career in anthropology, but the papers I published and presented at conferences gradually became less about Swiss peasants and more about what was coming to be called corporate anthropology. I did learn very quickly, though, not to present myself to the corporate world as an anthropologist. That seemed to suggest to many of our clients the nastier connotations of *academic:* pedantic, abstract, unrealistic, and impractical, as my thesaurus puts it so well. But my academic work as a university teacher was never "academic" in any of those senses.

It became even less so in the mid–1980s, when Jerry and I discovered Virginia Satir. She became such an enormous influence on both of us in our work. In 1989, teaming up with Jean McLendon, we designed and began teaching our next big workshop, the Congruent Leadership Change Shop. In the Change Shop, we translated Satir's amazing work with human families into the language and forms that fit well for corporate "families." Satir's term "family" was easily replaced with "team," and we three—Jerry, Jean, and I—became both a team and a family.

New Mexico

We moved to New Mexico in 1992 and, in the years since then, the fabric of our partnership began to take new forms. I moved into teaching people with dogs, and Jerry became a consultant's consultant and, most recently, a writer of science-fiction and fantasy novels. Jerry joined me as my silent partner in working with service dogs and their people, and I became the first reader of Jerry's novels. Both are positions of responsibility, high honor, and privilege. And so the partnership that "wouldn't last" seems to be gaining in longevity.

I have skipped very lightly over these forty-six years of partnership. Of course, there is much more: things we did together and things we did separately. As I look back, though, I think that PSL and the Change Shop embraced all of it—the good, the bad, the ugly, and the beautiful. We were a team, and we were more than a team. Our togetherness was inclusive, not exclusive, of other people. Our clients and students have also been our friends. Working together and being together do not seem like opposites, and I cannot think of anyone we consider a close friend with whom we have not done some kind of work. In fact, some of our best friends now team with Jerry to teach an occasional PSL, while I continue to immerse myself in my dog world.

At the same time, though, we do still live in a two-person dream world. In our early years together, Jerry used to daydream that we would buy an RV and travel around the world, giving workshops. This morning, though, he described a dream he had last night. We were once again leading PSL. Fifty people showed up, instead of our limit of twenty, and we didn't know what to do. We certainly didn't want to turn anyone away, so we decided to split the group between us. Jerry seemed pleased as he went about his breakfast.

And so we're still working, still solving problems, and still partners in our dreams and in our dream world.

15

Time—and How to Get It

Bent Adsersen

Many years ago, at our first workshop together, Jerry Weinberg reminded me that time is the most important gift you can give to other people. In honor of all the time that Jerry has given to me and so many others, I'd like to mark the occasion of Jerry's seventy-fifth birthday to explore the gift of time and what *time* means.

Before reading further, write down *your* definition of time on a piece of paper. What is *time*, really?

Was that easy or hard for you? Did it leave you wondering?

I have met many definitions, some of them very beautiful and thoughtful. But I have yet to meet a person able to articulate a definition that fully covers the concept in one sentence. That fact has always amazed me.

When I was a child, I tried to see how short a moment could be. Was it just a second? Or was it less than a second? I remember how I tried until my head almost hurt. I nearly drove myself insane. Relaxing afterward, I remember the way the seconds just ticked away from me: tick, tick, tick . . .

Many years after these experiments, I was exposed to the turmoil of organizational life. I noticed weird contradictions around time usage. I was confronted with frequent use of sentences like "We have no time for that" and "I can't find time to help you with this." In general, time seemed to be a very scarce resource. As my organizational experiences expanded, I found out that there would always be ample time for rework, while never enough time to do things right on the first attempt. What was this about?

Much later, on a vacation in Ireland, I recall being exposed to and aware of a totally different reality. I was traveling by boat, and the cruise was subject to a speed limit of five miles per hour. That was a very different experience. Slow time, you may call it. An Irish proverb claims, "When God created time, he created plenty of it." Yet my car trip back to the airport was in striking contrast. The car rushed along at more than thirty miles per hour, an astonishing speed compared to my weeks on the river. The cows in the fields went by in a blur.

Reflecting on these observations, I discovered that time, for sure, is a strange concept: Call it a quantity or a quality—it's a multidimensional contradiction.

Ways of Defining Time

In everyday life, we take time for granted and do not reflect on its definition. It is just a common, generally accepted thing. Reflecting more deeply, we realize that time is not that simple.

Here is a variety of responses I've received to my request for a definition:

> Time is impossible to define.
>
> Time consists of many different units.
>
> Time is nature's way of securing that everything does not happen at the same time.
>
> Time is what happens to me during my lifetime.
>
> Time is something I never have enough of.
>
> Time is the only thing I have.
>
> Time is a constraint.
>
> Time is measurable units.
>
> Time is a fourth dimension in space.
>
> Time is a circular loop; it will always come back to you.
>
> Time cannot be defined in itself.
>
> Time is a container, and you should be very cautious what to put in it.
>
> Time is a while.

Time is a quality.

Time is a dream.

Time is a space in which stuff happens.

And of course there is the official definition, used by science, in which the units for time are seconds—with time defined by the duration of a certain nuclear event multiplied by 9,192,631,770. The days of using the Earth's orbit around the sun are now in the past; we rely on greater accuracy than that.

In the efficient society in which we live, we are likely to depend on this last definition. Time is exact; time is structured. There is a need for accuracy in planning. There is a need to measure effort.

One is likely to forget that some events don't repeat in structured intervals. Babies enter this world on their birthday. Projects do, too. But we do not celebrate the babies' due dates before they are actually born.

Going back in history, we can trace the use of clocks and the need for clocks and efficiency. Today, everyone is likely to be in possession of numerous clocks. The current time is available everywhere, ticking away on any television, computer, or cell phone. In every airport, passengers are met with endless rows of ON TIME (if they're lucky).

In the medieval age, there were only one or two clocks in the village: one at the church and one on the town hall. The bells chimed every morning and every evening, notifying the peasants of the beginning of the work day and the end of the work day.

Going back further, there were no clocks at all in many cultures. How can it be possible to live in a society without clocks?

In ancient Greece, time was referred to by three terms: *Chaos, Chronos,* and *Kairos.*

Chaos was—well—just chaos. No structure, turmoil. No sense, you may say. Or maybe the contrary, maybe some sense in itself.

Chronos was order in a structural sense. Order, regularity, predictability.

> *Kairos* was the sacred room or sacred space, in which things could happen. Your own private space. Or you could share a space with others.

And time—and life—consisted of a combination of these three elements.

If you are really in *kairos*, you pay no attention to *chronos*. And if you pay attention to *chronos* only, you are likely to miss having any *kairos* at all.

Taken to the extreme, the full presence of either dimension eliminates the other. How much can you achieve in a person-month? A person-week? A person-hour? A person-minute? A person-second? Well, you can't rely on the last one in a structured sense, but you can actually achieve a lot in a golden, miraculous second. But such seconds are not likely to appear on command.

Chronos is an external attribute, as opposed to *kairos*, which is internal. *Chronos* can be used to measure the outside world, while *kairos* is beyond measurements—it is an internal state of mind.

How will you grasp the difference between the two?

A *chronos*-driven approach will be supported by motion, concentration, steering, pulse, and very rhythmic music.

A *kairos*-driven approach will be supported by emotion, openness, meditation, and soft, floating music.

Rhythm seems to be the essence here. You might call it "fast time" and "slow time." Many activities will have a desirable state to be performed in, a certain state most likely to be individual. Some activities will only be possible in either one state or the other.

If you are into classical music, listen to the fast, third movement of Beethoven's "Moonlight" sonata (Piano Sonata #14 in C Sharp Minor), followed by the slow, second movement of "The Elvira Madigan" concerto by Mozart (Piano Concerto #21 in C Major). If you let yourself absorb the music, you will feel the difference. Be sure to include a break between the two pieces. They are from different worlds.

Substitute Words for Time

One of the remarkable things about time is our inability to define the word properly in everyday life. When I am confronted with a sentence like, "I don't have time," I become suspicious. Since time is always available, there is likely to be something else missing. The missing element is our substitute for time. Sometimes, it is our excuse for not having time.

Notice, as you go along, the use of the word *time* and consider what word it may be a substitute for. It is interesting to become aware of the words that you and others could use instead of *time*.

For example, insert any of the following words as a substitute for *time* in various expressions, to see if they make sense. Very often, you will be better served by using the substitute word:

Life

Energy

Space

Focus

Rhythm

Presence

Availability

Trust

Courage

Choice

Motivation

Opportunity

Priority

Money

And, of course, you may have your very own word for *time*.

The number of different meanings is fascinating. No wonder it is difficult to define the word itself. You may explore how much *chronos* or *kairos* is contained in each of the above.

Different people may react strongly to some of the substitute words, depending on their cultural habits, personal beliefs, or personal experience.

My own favorite substitute word is *life*. For me, *life* is the most fitting synonym for *time*. It seems to fit in any context, or almost any connection—at least any connection related to *kairos*. This substitution reminds me that time is the only thing I really own, and I try to treat it accordingly, that is, having respect for my own time, trying to use my own time well, and also having respect for other people's time. That is exactly how I would like to treat time, as if the word *life* were at stake.

Past, Present, and Future

The present is a mechanism that converts expectations into past experience. It may be perceived as a moment—a particular point with no linear extent. Or, it may be perceived as a space, a room, a *kairos*.

What is here and now is presence, experience, the possibility to make choices, and the possibility to act, be involved, or be absorbed.

Ahead of us lies the future, with its hopes, dreams, expectations, and worries.

Behind us lies the past, with its memories, past impressions, past experience, joys, and regrets.

And time itself moves us along an uninterrupted journey, putting the future into our backpack, our past.

Everything we do happens in the present. We are captured in the present, in a particular *kairos*. It can feel tiny, it can feel big, but we are in it. We cannot reach out for the future or reach back to the past. You cannot change things in the past, but you can spoil the present by worrying about the future. We can only make decisions, take action, or change things in the present. *Carpe diem:* Seize the day. The day is basically all there is!

The present and the past exist only in our imagination. The future is our picture of the present, as looked upon through our present frame of reference. And the past, likewise, is our picture of what has happened, looked upon by the pair of glasses we wear today. What is interesting is that our pictures of the past and of the future will change as we move along in time.

What Time Does to You

Time can be viewed as something that happens to you.

When watching an analog clock, you notice the movement of the seconds. These clocks are made to make a physical measurement, controlled by oscillation, pulse, or pendulum. This is a very visible and direct way of expressing how time passes by.

Another, but slower, way is to notice the process of aging. It dosen't show from day to day, but you may suddenly notice that things have changed. Physical things that once were easy may not be so easy any more.

A third, also slower, way is to notice the way society changes over time. About a hundred years ago, cars and telephones were new inventions, and only a few people believed that practically anyone would be in possession of such things. It is not many years since e-mail and cell phones appeared. Today, it is hard to imagine a working society without these inventions. A few years ago, you may have asked, "Do you have an e-mail address?" Today, it is taken for granted. Culture is constantly changing. Some things change very fast, and some things change very slowly, but there will be differences in every epoch of history.

Sitting back and noticing time passing is a very inactive occupation, leading to the belief that time is outside us and we cannot do anything about it. This belief may lead to a reactive attitude and may very well pave your way to sad reflections about everything being perishable.

What You Can Do to Time

Time can also be viewed as something you do. Time is what we do.

I can do stuff. I can stand still. I can run fast. I can bore myself. I can entertain myself. I can encounter things. I can experience things. I can be together with friends or loved ones.

Viewing time in this way is very energizing. I can spend my time doing things that work for me. Time disappears as something that just happens to me. Inside, I experience that time spent on things I like seems to rush away, while time spent on boring things passes *veeeery* slowly. An hour with a good friend is gone in a minute, while a PowerPoint presentation can feel endless, even if it ends after twenty minutes. But I have a choice. I can do what is purposeful for me, and I can walk away from other things.

Viewing time as something you do leads to a belief that you can actually control time—by doing what you want. This is a proactive point of view, which may give hope, give new energy, and refresh your optimism.

The Danish philosopher Søren Kierkegaard exhibited this line of thinking when he wrote, "What is truth, but living for your idea?"

Choosing the Best Illusion

Now here is another question for you: Would you like to have more time available?

A genuine obstacle to having enough time is the common belief that there is too little time available. So we have to *hurry*. A lot of people are likely to have told you this: parents, older brothers and sisters, teachers, managers, executives. Not to mention people selling time-saving devices or services, such as portable computers, mobile phones, air travel, and so forth.

But did you get more time?

A classic Danish comedy shows a ridiculous person, Mr. Vielgeschrey, who is so absorbed in hurrying that he doesn't get anything done at all. The name itself translates to something like Mr. Much-Scream-and-Fuss. Many people relate to him when they watch the comedy. The humor feels very up-to-date. However, it was written in 1726. Not much has changed in terms of basic human mechanisms, except that we may be under greater stress from information-supporting devices these days.

A wonderful story on how to achieve more time is told by Bodil Jönsson, a physics professor at the University of Lund in Sweden: As the person responsible for research and student education, Bodil decided to spend some time figuring out the next term's research areas and curriculum. She gave her secretary instructions to block all interruptions for a full afternoon.

Coming back from her time thinking, she met her secretary, who was very distressed and almost in tears. "But my dear, what has happened to you?" Bodil asked.

"Oh, people have been so awful to me. Every time I said, 'But you cannot speak to Professor Jönsson right now, she is thinking today,' the immediate reaction was, '*What*? If this lady has nothing better to do, she could at least talk to *me!*'"

Bodil became very angry at the nastiness with which her secretary had been confronted. But she also started to think about her own behavior. She became aware that she lived a life with too little time for everything. After a period of speculation, she made an ingenious observation. Realizing that she had spent some forty years having too little time for everything, she said to herself, "If I am able to make myself believe that I don't have time for anything, then I must also be able to make myself believe that I have time for everything that I want."

That was her great discovery. Having too little time or having too much time: Both views are illusions. So, why not take advantage and choose the illusion you prefer?

Bodil did. She immediately took a two-month leave from her duties.

Not all of us are in a situation where we can do as Bodil did. Or are we? Choosing to work under certain conditions is a choice. Making choices has consequences, of course, but not making choices also has consequences—we're just not as likely to be aware of them.

There are days when I go to work with the intent of zipping through my work because I have so much to do. There are also the more-rare days, when I go to work with the intent of taking things slightly more calmly. If I compare the two types of day, I am astonished to find that the days when I actually get things done are the calm days.

There is a universal truth about time: The more you save, the less you get. The more you put effort into smaller and smaller chunks of time, the less time you have available. It is the *chronos-kairos* paradox. The Swiss author Michael Ende describes it very beautifully in his book *Momo*. In this book, "grey men" try to persuade people to be highly efficient, to save time. And what happens? The more that people try to be efficient, the less time they get. Here is another good opportunity to reflect over substitute words for time.

So, in order to get more time—if that is your desire—there are a few skills you need to exercise.

You should be able to use and enjoy both fast time and slow time (interrupted time or uninterrupted time, you may say). Most of us are brought up to do things in fast time. Children are usually good at using slow time, but as they age, society teaches them that this is not appropriate. Many cultures have the good sense to rest after lunch, to have a solid break, including some sleep, to prepare for doing something purposeful in the afternoon. A few organizations have incorporated this concept into their corporate culture, calling it a "power nap." It has to be efficient, though. You don't want to tell a customer that Mr. X is having his afternoon nap.

It is not easy to switch between slow time and fast time if you have spent considerable time in one or the other. Moving directly from a stressful working environment to a quiet holiday could be just as painful as moving from a quiet holiday back to the pace of organizational life.

However, an awareness of the two states can make it possible to work with both and to switch more easily between the two states.

Saying no is another useful habit to exercise. If you are unable to say no, you cannot really say yes, either. Yes and no are interrelated. If you find it difficult to say no, then focus on what you say yes to, instead. That may lead to more easily saying no to what becomes unimportant.

Dealing with people who deeply believe that hurrying is the meaning of life is a third issue. Remind them of one of the most successful persons in history, the Roman emperor Augustus. He had this key to success: *Festina Lente!* This means "hurry slowly." Do not make haste.

And so, recalling Jerry's reminder that time is the most important gift you can give to other people, I add that it's also an important gift to yourself. If you are in a hurry, you will have no time for others, and in the end, no time left for yourself. I am ever-so-grateful to Jerry for his timely advice.

Endnotes

[1]See J. Bullock, G.M. Weinberg, and M. Benesh, eds., *Roundtable on Project Management: A SHAPE Forum Dialogue* (New York: Dorset House Publishing, 2001), and G.M. Weinberg, M. Benesh, and J. Bullock, eds., *Roundtable on Technical Leadership: A SHAPE Forum Dialogue* (New York: Dorset House Publishing, 2002).

[2]W.C. Hetzel, ed., *Program Test Methods* (Englewood Cliffs, N.J.: Prentice-Hall, 1973).

[3]Ibid.

[4]Ibid.

[5]Ibid.

[6]H.D. Leeds and G.M. Weinberg, *Computer Programming Fundamentals* (New York: McGraw-Hill, 1961).

[7]G.M. Weinberg, "Experiments in Problem Solving," Ph.D. Thesis, The University of Michigan, 1965, p. 234. See http://www.satisfice.com/articles/weinberg.pdf.

[8]Ibid., p. 45.

[9]G.M. Weinberg, "Natural Selection as Applied to Computers and Programs," *General Systems*, Vol. 15 (1970).

[10]T.W. Plum and G.M. Weinberg, "Teaching Structured Programming Attitudes, Even in APL, By Example," *Proceedings of the Fourth SIGCSE Technical Symposium on Computer Science Education: SIGCSE '74* (New York: ACM, 1974), pp. 133-43.

[11]G.M. Weinberg, *Quality Software Management, Vol. 1: Systems Thinking* (New York: Dorset House Publishing, 1992), p. 7.

[12]Quality Software, *TASSQ Magazine*, Vol. 4, No. 1 (Toronto: TASSQ, 2006).

[13]SHAPE Forum.

[14]M. McLuhan and B. Nevin, *Take Today: The Executive as Dropout* (New York: Harcourt Brace Jovanovich, 1972), p. 8.

[15]This recalls the wonderful title of Doris Lessing's book *Prisons We Choose to Live Inside*.

[16]K.E. Weick, *Sensemaking in Organizations* (Thousand Oaks, Calif.: Sage Publications, 1995), p. 89.

[17]M. Gladwell, *Blink: The Power of Thinking Without Thinking* (New York: Little, Brown and Company, 2005).

[18]Weick, op. cit., p. 56.

[19]B.V. Koen, *Discussion of the Method: Conducting the Engineer's Approach to Problem Solving* (New York: Oxford University Press, 2003).

[20]In *Discussion of the Method*, Koen uses a typographical convention, underlining the second letter of words that need to be treated as uncertain, relative to some person, to remind us when we're dealing with a heuristic. His conclusion: All is heuristic.

[21]See J. Bach's essay, immediately preceding in this volume.

[22]V. Satir, *Peoplemaking* (Palo Alto, Calif.: Science and Behavior Books, 1972).

[23]R. Blake and J. Mouton's Managerial Grid Model (1964) is a model for behavioral leadership, which identifies five different leadership styles based on the *concern for people* and the *concern for production*. (See: http://en.wikipedia.org/wiki/Managerial_Grid_Model)

[24]The Myers-Briggs Type Indicator (MBTI) is a personality assessment tool developed more than fifty years ago by Isabel Briggs Myers and her mother, Katharine Briggs, who extended the ideas

and theories of Carl Jung, putting the concepts into language more easily understood.

[25]P.G. Burnham, *Playtraining Your Dog* (New York: St. Martin's Griffin, 1985).

[26]G.M. Weinberg wrote about some of his favorite tools in *More Secrets of Consulting: The Consultant's Tool Kit* (New York: Dorset House Publishing, 2001).

[27]C. Seashore, E.W. Seashore, and G.M. Weinberg, *What Did You Say? The Art of Giving and Receiving Feedback* (Columbia, Md.: Bingham House Books, 1997).

[28]For specifics pertaining to Satir's model, see V. Satir et al., *The Satir Model: Family Therapy and Beyond* (Palo Alto, Calif.: Science and Behavior Books, 1991) and G.M. Weinberg, *Quality Software Management: Vol. 3, Congruent Action* (New York: Dorset House Publishing, 1994).

[29]V. Satir et al., *The Satir Model: Family Therapy and Beyond* (Palo Alto, Calif.: Science and Behavior Books, 1991).

[30]Ibid., p. 66.

[31]http://en.wikipedia.org/wiki/Groupthink, July 7, 2008.

[32]G.M. Weinberg, *Quality Software Management, Vol. 3: Congruent Action* (New York: Dorset House Publishing, 1994), pp. 26-28.

[33]Ibid., p. 111.

[34]Nynke Fokma, Marc Evers, Fiona Charles, and two anonymous reviewers gave invaluable constructive comments on an early draft of this essay—my thanks to each.

[35]M.A. Jackson, *Principles of Program Design* (London: Academic Press, 1975).

[36]G.M. Weinberg, *Weinberg on Writing: The Fieldstone Method* (New York: Dorset House Publishing, 2006), pp. 14ff.

[37]Ibid., p. 6.

[38]Ibid., pp. 125-26.

[39]G.M. Weinberg, *Quality Software Management, Vol. 3: Congruent Action* (New York: Dorset House Publishing, 1994).

[40]S. McConnell, *Code Complete: A Practical Handbook of Software Construction* (Redmond, Wash.: Microsoft Press, 1993).

[41]J. Spolsky, "There's No Place Like 127.0.0.1" (http://www.joelon software.com/items/2007/09/11.html, 2007).

[42]K. Beck, "Gerald Weinberg" (http://c2.com/cgi/wiki?GeraldWe inberg).

[43]J. Bach "Recommended Reading" (http://www.satisfice.com/bi bliography.shtml).

[44]D.H. Hansson, "Preserving Survival Rules in Face of Enthu- siasm" (http://www.loudthinking.com/arc/000469.html, 2007).

[45]Ibid., personal correspondence, December 2007.

[46]M. Gladwell, *The Tipping Point: How Little Things Can Make a Big Difference* (Boston: Back Bay Publishing, 2002).

[47]G.M. Weinberg, personal correspondence, December 2006.

[48]G.M. Weinberg, *The Secrets of Consulting: A Guide to Giving and Getting Advice Successfully* (New York: Dorset House Publishing, 1985), p. 1.

Bibliography

Chronological List of Books by Gerald M. Weinberg

Computer Programming Fundamentals, with H.D. Leeds. New York: McGraw-Hill, 1961.

Experiments in Problem Solving, doctoral thesis. Ann Arbor, Mich.: University Microfilms, 1965.

PL/I Programming Primer. New York: McGraw-Hill, 1966.

Computer Programming Fundamentals Based on the IBM System 360, with H.D. Leeds. New York: McGraw-Hill, 1970.

PL/I Programming. New York: McGraw-Hill, 1970.

The Psychology of Computer Programming. New York: Van Nostrand Reinhold, 1971. (Silver Anniversary ed., New York: Dorset House Publishing, 1998)

Structured Programming in PL/C, with N.F. Yasakawa and R. Marcus. New York: John Wiley & Sons, 1973.

Teacher's Guide to Structured Programming in PL/C, with N.F. Yasakawa and R. Marcus. New York: John Wiley & Sons, 1973.

An Introduction to General Systems Thinking. New York: John Wiley & Sons, 1975. (New York: Dorset House Publishing, 2001)

Humanized Input, with T. Gilb. Cambridge, Mass.: Winthrop Publishing, 1976.

High-Level COBOL Programming, with S. Wright, R. Kauffman, and M. Goetz. Cambridge, Mass.: Winthrop Publishing,1977.

147

Are Your Lights On? with D.C. Gause. Cambridge, Mass.: Winthrop Publishing, 1982. (Reprint, New York: Dorset House Publishing, 1990.)

On the Design of Stable Systems, with D. Weinberg. New York: John Wiley & Sons, 1979.

Handbook of Walkthroughs, Inspections, and Technical Reviews, 3rd ed., with D. Freedman. Boston: Little, Brown and Company, 1982. (Reprint, New York: Dorset House Publishing, 1990)

Rethinking Systems Analysis and Design. Boston: Little, Brown and Company, 1982. (Reprint, New York: Dorset House Publishing, 1988)

Understanding the Professional Programmer. Boston: Little, Brown and Company, 1982. (Reprint, New York: Dorset House Publishing, 1988)

Computer Information Systems, with D. Geller. Boston: Little, Brown and Company, 1985.

The Secrets of Consulting. New York: Dorset House Publishing, 1985.

Becoming a Technical Leader. New York: Dorset House Publishing, 1986.

General Principles of Systems Design, with D. Weinberg. New York: Dorset House Publishing, 1988. (Originally titled *On the Design of Stable Systems*)

Exploring Requirements, with D.C. Gause. New York: Dorset House Publishing, 1989.

What Did You Say? with E.W. Seashore and C. Seashore. Columbia, Md.: Bingham House Books, 1991.

Quality Software Management, Vol. 1: Systems Thinking. New York: Dorset House Publishing, 1991.

Quality Software Management, Vol. 2: First Order Measurement. New York: Dorset House Publishing, 1993.

Quality Software Management, Vol. 3: Congruent Action. New York: Dorset House Publishing, 1994.

Quality Software Management, Vol. 4: Anticipating Change. New York: Dorset House Publishing, 1997.

Amplifying Your Effectiveness, ed., with J. Bach and N. Karten. New York: Dorset House Publishing, 2000.

Roundtable on Project Management, ed., with J. Bullock and M. Benesh. New York: Dorset House Publishing, 2001.

More Secrets of Consulting. New York: Dorset House Publishing, 2002.

Roundtable on Technical Leadership, ed., with M. Benesh and J. Bullock. New York: Dorset House Publishing, 2002.

Weinberg on Writing. New York: Dorset House Publishing, 2006.

The Aremac Project. New York: Little West Press, 2007.

Perfect Software. New York: Dorset House Publishing, 2008.

Web Resources

Principal website: www.geraldmweinberg.com

Weinberg on Writing blog: http://weinbergonwriting.blogspot.com

Secrets of Consulting blog: http://secretsofconsulting.blogspot.com

AYE Conference: http://www.ayeconference.com

Additional Books, Articles, and Web Resources

Bach, J. "Recommended Reading." http://www.satisfice.com/bibliography.shtml.

Burnham, P.G. *Playtraining Your Dog.* New York: St. Martin's Griffin, 1985.

Draeger, D.F. *The Martial Arts and Ways of Japan,* 3 vols. New York: Weatherhill, 1973-74.

Gladwell, M. *Blink.* New York: Little, Brown and Company, 2005.

————, *The Tipping Point: How Little Things Can Make a Big Difference.* Boston, Mass.: Back Bay Publishing, 2002.

Hansson, D.H. "Preserving Survival Rules in Face of Enthusiasm." http://www.loudthinking.com/arc/000469.html, 2007.

Hetzel, W.C., ed. *Program Test Methods.* Englewood Cliffs, N.J.: Prentice-Hall, 1973.

Jackson, M.A. *Principles of Program Design.* London: Academic Press, 1975.

Koen, B.V. *Discussion of the Method.* New York: Oxford University Press, 2003.

McConnell, S. *Code Complete.* Redmond, Wash.: Microsoft Press, 1993.

McLuhan, M., and B. Nevin. *Take Today.* New York: Harcourt Brace Jovanovich, 1972.

Nicol, C.W. *Moving Zen.* New York: Harper Collins, 2001.

Plum, T.W., and G.M. Weinberg. "Teaching Structured Programming Attitudes, Even in APL, By Example." *Proceedings of the Fourth SIGCSE Technical Symposium on Computer Science Education: SIGCSE '74.* New York: ACM, 1974, pp. 133-43.

Satir, V. *Peoplemaking.* Palo Alto, Calif.: Science and Behavior Books, 1972.

————, et al. *The Satir Model.* Palo Alto, Calif.: Science and Behavior Books, 1991.

Weick, K.E. *Sensemaking in Organizations.* Thousand Oaks, Calif.: Sage Publications, 1995.

Spolsky, J. "There's No Place Like 127.0.0.1." (http://www.joelonsoftware.com/items/2007/09/11.html, 2007.

Weinberg, G.M. "Natural Selection as Applied to Computers and Programs." *General Systems,* Vol. 15 (1970).

Westbrook, A.M., and O. Ratti. *Aikido and the Dynamic Sphere.* Boston: Tuttle Publishing, 1970.

Contributor
Biographies

BENT ADSERSEN **bentadsersen@compuserve.com**

Bent Adsersen is an independent Danish project consultant. Bent entered the software business in 1973 and realized soon that software development was basically about people making useful stuff for other people. After a decade of developing systems, he started conducting experiential learning exercises and project retrospectives to give fellow developers insight into the processes actually going on.

In 1994, Bent left organizational life to become a freelance consultant. His special interests include teaching end users and nontechnical people how to make useful requirements and how to perform proper software testing. He also coaches technical people and managers how to guide meaningful organizational changes.

During his career, Bent has been in touch with projects throughout the world. He has helped numerous projects in various environments, mostly in Scandinavia, bringing theory into practice by adding to skills already present. He has trained thousands of students through experiential learning sessions.

JAMES BACH **james@satisfice.com**

James Bach travels the world teaching software testing as a martial art of the mind. Starting as a video game programmer after dropping out of high school, he later became the youngest manager at Apple Computer, in 1987. Since then, he's worked at several Silicon Valley companies, consulted and developed a methodology for rapidly testing software, and served as an expert witness. An authority on the exploratory approach to testing and a founder of the Context-Driven School of testing, he is coauthor of *Lessons*

Learned in Software Testing, as well as author of a forthcoming book about self-education, *Secrets of a Buccaneer Scholar.*

MICHAEL BOLTON   mb@developsense.com

Michael Bolton has taught software testing on five continents for eight years. He is coauthor (with James Bach) of Rapid Software Testing, a course which presents a methodology and mindset for testing software expertly in uncertain conditions and under extreme time pressure. He is program chair for Toronto Association of System and Software Quality (TASSQ) conference, and a cofounder of Toronto Workshop on Software Testing. He is a regular contributor to *Better Software* and TASSQ's *Quality Software* magazines, and very sporadically produces his own newsletter. Michael lives in Toronto, with his wife and two children.

JAMES BULLOCK   jbullock@rare-bird-ent.com

Jim Bullock is a development consultant who helps people ship when they couldn't, deliver better and faster versus worse and slower, and build things that were previously beyond their reach. He performs "conscious development," helping people to notice and tune how they build software to provide the product and delivery they need.

Jim particularly values Jerry's insight into how things work, especially in the context of people thinking together under pressure and in the profoundly human endeavor of building software.

An editor of the *Roundtable* series, Jim is currently writing about how change happens in technology development organizations.

FIONA CHARLES   Fiona.charles@quality-intelligence.com

Fiona Charles teaches organizations to match their software testing to their business risks and opportunities. Working in software development since 1978, Fiona began as a technical writer and graduated into testing, quality assurance, test management, and test consulting. She has made a specialty of managing—and teaching others to manage—enterprise-wide integration tests across multiple systems and platforms, motivating people from disparate organizational cultures to work together in an effective integrated test. She also specializes in rescuing stalled testing projects, rebuilding and inspiring teams to focus on testing that matters to stakeholders.

Throughout her career, Fiona has advocated, designed, implemented, and taught pragmatic and humane practices to deliver software worth having, in even the most difficult project circumstances. Her articles on testing and test management appear frequently in *Better Software* magazine and on StickyMinds.com. She is a cofounder and host of Toronto Workshop on Software Testing.

ESTHER DERBY   **derby@estherderby.com**
Esther Derby is founder of Esther Derby Associates, a consulting firm dedicated to helping teams and managers reach new levels of productivity, offering clients expertise, a pragmatic approach, and an ability to reframe difficult interactions toward creative possibilities. She works with Fortune 500 firms as well as small, niche-market firms.

Esther leads workshops and speaks internationally. She is a regular contributor to *Better Software, Software Development, CrossTalk,* and, online, ayeconference.com, cio.com, sticky minds.com, and scrumalliance.org. She is coauthor of *Agile Retrospectives* (with Diana Larsen) and *Behind Closed Doors* (with Johanna Rothman). Esther has an M.A. in organizational leadership.

ROBERT L. GLASS   **rlglass@acm.org**
Robert Glass is president of Computing Trends and editor and publisher of *The Software Practitioner* newsletter. He is a guest professor of software engineering at Griffith University, Brisbane, Australia.

Bob has been active in the field of computing and software for more than fifty years, largely in industry but also in academia. He is author of nearly thirty books and ninety papers on computing subjects, editor emeritus of Elsevier's *Journal of Systems and Software,* and a columnist for several periodicals including *IEEE Software* and *Information Systems Management.* He has served as an ACM Lecturer and an ACM fellow. In 1995, he received an honorary doctorate from Linkoping University in Sweden.

SHERRY HEINZE   sheinze@telusplanet.net

Sherry Heinze has more than twenty-five years of information technology experience as a tester, trainer, analyst, and technical writer, with a broad background in design, testing, implementation, training, documentation, and user support. Sherry added to her skillset in Weinberg and Weinberg's Problem Solving Leadership workshop in 2002, and in their Consulting Skills workshop in 2006. She has participated in the annual Amplifying Your Effectiveness conference since it began in 2000. Sherry also is a member of the board of the Virginia Satir Global Network.

NAOMI KARTEN   Naomi@nkarten.com

Naomi Karten has delivered seminars and presentations to more than 100,000 people internationally to help them improve customer satisfaction, manage change, strengthen teamwork, and improve communication skills. Her books *Managing Expectations* and *Communication Gaps and How to Close Them* provide proven strategies and techniques for carrying out projects, implementing change, delivering superior service, and building strong relationships.

Naomi's e-books include *How to Establish Service-Level Agreements* and *How to Survive, Excel and Advance as an Introvert.* Her online newsletter *Perceptions & Realities,* which is posted on her Website, offers serious advice in a lively, chuckle-generating manner. She has also published more than three hundred articles in print and on numerous Websites.

Prior to forming her training and consulting business in 1984, Naomi earned bachelor's and master's degrees in psychology and gained extensive experience in technical, customer support, and management positions.

JONATHAN KOHL   jonathan@kohl.ca

Jonathan Kohl is a consultant, author, and speaker in the software industry. Since 1998, he has worked on a variety of software development projects, primarily as a software tester, and as a business analyst, technical writer, and programmer. He trains and mentors software testers to improve their skills.

Jonathan is a popular blogger on software testing and software development issues and is author of more than a dozen articles. He is a frequent contributor to *Better Software* magazine, both as an author and technical editor, and speaks on software-related topics at user groups, workshops, and software conferences.

Based in Calgary, Jonathan is a cofounder and principal consultant of Kohl Concepts, a software-services consulting company. He lives in Calgary with his wife, Elizabeth, and their border collie, Heidi.

TIM LISTER   lister@acm.org

Tim Lister is a software consultant for the Atlantic Systems Guild, based in New York. He divides his time between consulting, teaching, and writing. He is coauthor of *Adrenaline Junkies and Template Zombies; Waltzing With Bears,* winner of *Software Development* magazine's Jolt Award as General Computing Book of the Year for 2003-2004; and *Peopleware,* now available in fourteen languages.

Tim is a member of the Cutter IT Trends Council, the IEEE, and the ACM. He is in his twenty-third year as a panelist for the American Arbitration Association, specializing in arbitration of disputes involving software and software services.

JEAN A. MCLENDON, LCSW, LMFT   jmclendon@satirsystems.com

Jean McLendon is recognized nationally and internationally for her broad application of the methods and concepts of the Satir Growth Model. Based in Chapel Hill, N.C., she travels extensively, presenting in the areas of clinical, personal, organizational, and leadership development. She is past president of the Virginia Satir Global Network (formerly Avanta) and is a founding director of training for the Satir Institute of the Southeast. Her clinical work is featured in Allyn & Bacon's video series "Family Therapy with the Experts." She is a frequent conference keynote and is author of journal articles and book chapters for both clinical and organizational professional publications.

JUDAH MOGILENSKY   judah@pep-inc.com

Judah Mogilensky is an owner and partner of Process Enhancement Partners, providing process improvement support to commercial and government clients throughout the United States, Canada, Europe, Israel, and the Far East, as a consultant, trainer, and appraisal team leader. He is a SCAMPI High Maturity Lead Appraiser, an authorized instructor for the SEI's Introduction to the CMM course, and a SCAMPI Lead Appraiser for the People CMM.

Judah serves as a Visiting Scientist at the SEI, performing as a SCAMPI-A Observer and a High Maturity Lead Appraiser examiner, and is a proud member of the 1996-97 Satir System Training class. In 1998, he served as an apprentice at Congruent Change Shop and has also served two terms as Consultants' Camp Leader. He holds B.S. and M.S. degrees in electrical engineering from Cornell University.

Sue Petersen suep@cowgirlcoder.com

Sue Petersen is an anthropologist by training, a programmer by avocation, and a manager by necessity. With her husband, she owns and operates a plumbing repair shop in Oregon.

Sue began training with Jerry Weinberg in 1995, and remains a firm believer that "It's people-stuff all the way down!"

Sue began her career as a professional writer when she sold her first article to *Windows Tech Journal* in 1995. She wrote a book-review column for *Visual Developer* magazine for many years and continues to freelance for industry publications.

Johanna Rothman jr@jrothman.com

Johanna Rothman helps leaders and managers solve problems and seize opportunities. She consults, speaks, and writes on managing high-technology product development. She enables managers, teams, and organizations to become more effective by applying her pragmatic approaches to the issues of project management, risk management, and people management.

Johanna writes and publishes *The Pragmatic Manager,* a close-to-monthly e-mail newsletter, and two blogs, Managing Product Development and Hiring Technical People. Her books include *Manage It!; Behind Closed Doors* (with Esther Derby); *Hiring the Best Knowledge Workers, Techies & Nerds;* and *Corrective Action for the Software Industry* (with Denise Robitaille). Her many articles are available on her Website and a forthcoming book on project portfolio management will be published in 2009.

WILLEM VAN DEN ENDE   **willem@willemvandenende.com**

Willem van den Ende has been puzzled by people's behavior, especially in groups, for as long as he can remember. He's especially interested in finding more humane and sustainable ways of developing software. He is an entrepreneur, based in the Netherlands, who works around the world as an all-hands person developing software, mentoring teams, and delivering courses that make a difference in everyday life.

Willem is an active software community member, speaking regularly at conferences, and is cofounder of XP Days Benelux and the Agile Open Conference series, a cohost of systemsthinking.net, and a former board member for Agile Alliance. Willem's sharp vision, broad knowledge, and twenty years of experience as programmer and coach enable him to adopt an improvising attitude during workshops, enabling people to see things differently.

DANI WEINBERG   **daniw@earthlink.net**

Dani Weinberg is a dog trainer, dog behavior consultant, and a trainers' trainer. Formerly a university professor and applied anthropologist, her current professional life in the world of dogs allows her to pursue her lifelong interests in learning and communication. She uses human models of learning and communication to help people enhance their relationships with their dogs. In her previous life as an anthropologist and organizational consultant, she published *Peasant Wisdom: Cultural Adaptation in a Swiss Village* and coauthored (with G.M. Weinberg) *General Principles of Systems Design.* Her most recent work with people and their dogs is detailed in her book *Teaching People Teaching Dogs.*

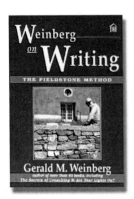